The Art of Healing
from Sexual Trauma

The Art of Healing
from Sexual Trauma

Tending Body and Soul through Creativity, Nature, and Intuition

Naomi Ardea

This book is intended to further general knowledge and understanding of sexual trauma and the conditions experienced by persons who have been subjected to sexual trauma. This book is not meant to be used, nor should it be used, to diagnose or treat any physical or mental health condition. It is not intended to serve as and should not be relied upon as recommending or promoting any specific remedies, practices, or procedures, and it is not intended as a substitute for advice from a qualified health care professional. The publisher and author are not responsible for any specific health or allergy needs that may require medical supervision and are not liable for any damages or negative consequences that may result from following any technique or practice discussed herein. References are provided for informational purposes only and do not constitute endorsement of any websites or other sources.

ISBN 13: 978-1-63489-915-4
eISBN 13: 978-1-63489-914-7

Library of Congress Catalog Number: 2016937264
Printed in the United States of America
First Printing: 2016

20 19 18 17 16   5 4 3 2 1

Cover and interior design by Ryan Scheife, Mayfly Design

Minneapolis, MN
www.wiseinkpub.com

To order, visit www.seattlebookcompany.com or call (734) 426-6248. Reseller discounts available.

For my sister and my son,
for helping me remember the little girl who loved to play

Medical Note

The ideas, practices, and self-care techniques presented in this book are not a form of, or a substitute for, professional psychotherapy or medical care. If you are experiencing symptoms of trauma, you may need to consult qualified professional help. If you choose to perform these self-care techniques on your own, and if you experience physical or emotional reactions that feel too intense to manage, you should seek professional help. Primary care physicians, rape crisis centers, and social service organizations may provide referrals for psychotherapy or other professional help.

Table of Contents

Safe Table of Contents

Find pages with "safe" content (without common triggers, including abuse, psychological trauma, etc.) by looking for 🌿 above page numbers

Introduction

This takes courage. Within these pages, I share deeply personal details about what healing from sexual abuse has looked like for me. I am one of those one-in-four women who has been sexually abused. One-in-six men have been sexually abused. I'm shocked by these frequently quoted statistics.

How did I grow up with so little understanding of sexual abuse?

It's everywhere, indirectly or directly affecting us. Why was it so hard to find good help when a professional mentor crossed sexual boundaries with me? Why did I feel so alone and confused as I uncovered my own childhood sexual abuse history?

The answer is simple. So few people talk about sexual abuse, and few people share details from their moment-by-moment, day-by-day healing journeys.

I feel compelled to step up and fill a portion of this void with my words, paintings, photographs, and healing experiences. I hope these personal expressions will deepen the understanding of others and give clarity to the impact of sexual abuse. These truths need to exist in the open, beyond therapy rooms, private journals, and online victim support forums. As a society, we need to support and advocate for those who have been hurt.

I wrote this book with myself in mind as well. It is healing for me to imagine giving a copy of this book to the distraught woman I was many years ago. I'd tell her to trust her feelings and to keep listening for her own inner voice for guidance on how she can heal her wounds. I'd want her to know that's how she came to be writing this book to help herself and others.

I'm disheartened that, for legal reasons, I'm unable to share more information about the abuses I've lived through. In order to publish while my abusers are still living, the details would have to be altered, which felt exhausting and dishonest.

However, the aftermath I describe is the truth, as are the healing practices I've adopted.

I offer my experiences to encourage others to share. Together, unsilenced, we can heal.

Trauma in Me

Our bodies are our psyches, our souls. Sexual violation reverberates to the core of our physical bodies and impacts much more of our lives than just our sexualities. A person's sense of self can become damaged by sexual abuse. Shame, self-blame, and low self-worth seem to be the psyche's way of communicating about the invisible wounds, especially in a society where victims are sometimes neither believed nor encouraged to be open about their distress. Emotional numbing, emotional flooding, decreased physical awareness, and loss of trust are some of the ways we cope when the wounds aren't tended. Our bodies hold these internal injuries as tension, imbalance, pain, and illness.

I was not prepared to be an advocate for my own healing. I'd accepted my lifelong patterns of anxiety and recurring depression as part of who I was. When these patterns intensified, I had no idea that listening more closely to them would uncover childhood sexual abuse. I didn't understand that sexualization by a professional mentor is abuse as well. I hadn't anticipated that as my son grew, my unhealed pain from when I was his age would emerge, asking for my care.

Exhausted, I survived within my shaky self, sure I'd done something wrong. The world invaded and overpowered me.

My training and experience as a massage therapist has taught me that emotions can lie at the root of unease in our bodies. Still, when my own body began telling me how violated I had been—and still was—I was shocked. A part of me knew that I needed to keep listening to my body. Psychotherapy gave me the freedom to talk about my experience, emotions, and thoughts; isn't that how people recover from anxiety and depression, both of which I experienced regularly? While talk therapy offered many benefits, I had so much more work to do. Looking back, I wish I had understood more about healing from sexual trauma. I didn't know what questions to ask, what was normal, or what a healing path might look like.

Becoming solid and comfortable in my own skin has been a long, difficult road. I consulted body-oriented therapists, talk therapists, and doctors. Diagnoses of generalized anxiety, post-traumatic stress disorder (PTSD), chronic pain, chronic fatigue, and sensory processing disorder best fit my symptoms. I took medications and herbs. I read and skimmed scores of books about sexual violation and trauma. I developed self-care techniques to soothe my fried nervous system. Eventually, I grasped what healing meant to me and my body. Finding a healing path doesn't have to be confusing. We need more victims to raise their voices and share details of their inner lives.

I can share from my inner life. I can share what I've learned about trauma healing and what helps me.

The core of this book contains a series of eleven chapters. Each chapter offers a view into a key theme of my healing journey. This view is composed of some or all of these elements:

My Paintings & Reflections   Survivor's Toolbox
Healing Episodes   Open Space
Key Theme Discussion   Photographic Pauses
Creative Self-Care

My Paintings & Reflections

I introduce the core chapters with my paintings. During the chaos of several intense years, I reconnected with deeply feeling and expressive parts of my spirit. Painting is a healing balm for me. Somehow, the intensity of what I feel travels out of me through my hands and into the paint. This art was born from pain, betrayal, love, grief, panic, faith, and renewal.

Typically, my paintings emerge without much forethought. I choose colors based on what I'm drawn to at the time. Wearing latex gloves, I move the paint

A Healing Path

across the paper with my hands. Emotions flow in tandem. Painting isn't simply my means of documenting inner transformation; painting is a conduit for the transformative force itself. I sense that this vital force, what I think of as healing grace, still speaks within many of my paintings.

Swirling spirals, bursts, lines, and circles are patterns within my paintings as well as overall patterns of my healing pathway. I begin in darkness, with no clarity, dipping into turbulent waters, spinning up and out of my core, falling back into the pain, finding moments of peace, choosing to allow more pain to surface, feeling engulfed, floating more comfortably, finding roots, growing solidity in my core, feeling distress at descending again, sensing my life force draining, being shocked out of being in touch with my body, and eventually emerging with more confidence that I know how to tend these wounds when or if they reopen.

I painted more soothing images early on. It took a while before I wanted to see on paper what I was feeling inside. Many of the paintings had layers and layers of paint—I tended to cover the more disturbing patterns with soothing colors. *Small Me* (page 44), *Fear* (page 108), *Cradling Insanity* (page 80), *Get Out of Me* (page 106), and *Twisted* (page 132) emerged well into my healing journey, after I had more clear memories of childhood abuse. At that point, a shift toward self-validation allowed me the freedom to express those feelings. After I'd created the darker, creepier images, I'd usually put them away and view them sporadically. They were medicine I needed to take in small doses to avoid overdosing into dissociation, anxiety, nausea, or rage. *Cradling Insanity* still has the power to fill me with nausea. In fact, even uplifting images were too potent to display in the early phases of my healing. Now, I can spend time with most of the paintings without feeling turmoil.

I've come to see a progression in how I've expressed the impacts of abuse. I'd been silenced so forcefully that my psyche needed to repress memories to protect me and preserve some sanity by creating a more limited existence. Coming out of this stranglehold on my true voice began with abstract paintings. Through their creation, I could express what I'd endured, even before the repressed childhood abuse emerged into light and before I'd received strong validation that trusted professionals abuse clients when sexualizing the relationship. Painting felt safer than talking about my inner distress. It offered relief in navigating the flood of long-suppressed emotions. These images held the fullness and pain of my experiences before I could speak of them.

Gradually, I added words to my paintings. I kept most of these more vocal ones in hiding, as I did with the more disturbing work. Others would be more likely to doubt the truth of these more blatant expressions, and I wanted to avoid conflict—to avoid anything that might make someone blame me. So I colored the paper in what others might interpret as generalities.

Now I can see the foundation of self-acceptance and self-validation that these abstract paintings created for me. I spoke out in small steps, transitioning from privately creating and speaking to a few people about my experiences, to showing my paintings publicly and sharing my journey with you. A gradual and monumental shift occurred in me. Abstract self-validation shed layers of fear, allowing me to offer the truth.

Words do not always convey the fullness of the complex experiences. Images can silently speak volumes.

Healing Episodes

Within the core chapters, journal entries record the footprints of trauma. In these, I wrote about the overwhelming sensations, emotions, images, and thoughts related to past traumatic events. These experiences may have lasted minutes—or an afternoon, a full day, a week. The violence revisiting me rarely shows up in an easy-to-understand format like a movie. Usually it is experiential, as though my unhealed parts need me to feel and understand the pain again in order to let it go. Years of active—yet somewhat blind—healing came before clear visual and auditory memories emerged. Then, along with lifting self-blame from the more recent assaults, I could not deny my childhood abuse and trauma.

Here was a turning point that allowed me a new perspective on all that I'd been experiencing. I was no longer just a stressed-out spouse and mother who'd been considered "overly sensitive" by her family. Patterns emerged. Patterns of what triggers me. Patterns of pain. Patterns of emotions. Patterns of sensations. Patterns of thoughts. Patterns of how all this relates to the traumatic experiences. Hoping to resolve the recurring agony, I tracked the trajectories of these "healing episodes."

While I call them "healing episodes," for a long time I judged myself harshly about these experiences. *What's wrong with me? Why can't I just pull it together?* The judgment fell away as I researched PTSD, trauma triggers, and sensory body memories as part of the impacts of trauma. Early childhood traumas may only be experienced and resolved through the body since the early childhood brain does not record memories the same way that an older brain does.

Within these accounts, you will see examples of key elements in my trauma healing: deepening inner awareness, triggers, dissociation, self-blame, broken boundaries, reflowing emotions, and more. You'll also see examples of self-care techniques that over time have helped transform my pain into health.

This is my story. It's not linear because healing has not been linear. Rather, my journey progressed erratically as flooding and receding waves, protective coverings removed in strips, and caverns accidentally discovered. The past bubbles to the surface of the present.

Key Theme Discussion

These sections include my experiences and reflections on key phases and approaches of my healing from sexual trauma. I present these topics in an order that generally follows my own healing steps, yet phases will overlap. I revisit some, as though healing in a spiral, coming back to familiar themes over and over yet in a new way.

Creative Self-Care

For each key theme, I describe several self-care techniques I've found effective for that particular phase in healing. You'll find these techniques, as well as others, in more complete lists in the "Building a Foundation of Creative Self-Care" chapter toward the end of the book on page 155. I offer my self-care experiences with the hope that they may inspire you to try these techniques or create your own approaches to self-healing.

Survivor's Toolbox

These toolboxes provide detailed instructions for techniques and activities I've found helpful for my own healing.

Open Space

These journal pages offer room for your own expression. Many readers may feel a strong resistance to writing in a book. I ask that you give yourself permission to make this book your own. Fear not the open space. Use it to reflect on what a painting or photograph evokes within you. Sketch what you dreamed of last night. Write out your hopes and rants. Doodle. Color. Draw. Paste. Paint. Collage. It's okay if the pages wrinkle. Feel free to keep this book safely tucked away in order to let yourself be authentic. Create a conversation with the book. Write and draw in the margins on other pages. Your creativity will lead you into deeper healing.

Photographic Pauses

Between chapters, I offer my photographs to encourage you to pause. I find it useful to take breaks whenever reading about trauma. These photographs provide time for reflection and gentle breathing.

A Note about Word Choice

There is no consensus about what to call people who have suffered sexual violation. Victim? Survivor? Thriver? I've chosen to use terms that have felt appropriate for my own path, so you will see "victim" and "survivor" used in this book. I haven't felt that "thriver" suits me, but it may resonate with you.

I wish "victim" didn't have the negative association with wallowing—"being a victim" or "playing the victim card." I was a victim of crimes. I wouldn't judge someone for the speed of their healing from a physical assault; victims of sexual assault may carry invisible wounds for many years.

I feel some concern that society is pushing a "stronger" label of "survivor" or "thriver" onto victims in order to avoid seeing the painful damage they endure. I worry that the implied progression or hierarchy within these terms can rush people in healing, as they try desperately not to be a "victim" any longer. There is no weakness in feeling and tending deep pain. That said, I also encourage you to use the term that feels most honest and comfortable to you. Feel free to replace "victim" or "survivor" with your preferred term.

Walking through This Book

For those with PTSD, symptoms can include having difficulty with concentration. So I've created short sections, image pauses, and easily scanned lists as an intentional format for this book. Content that is more easily absorbed in small portions is also potentially less triggering. As you make your way through this book, I encourage you to periodically pause and turn your attention inward. This is especially vital for survivors of abuse. After looking at a painting or reading a journal entry, take time to notice and address any feelings that arise. Set the book aside, skip to the self-care sections, write about your present moment, or talk to a friend. Please seek professional help if your inner responses feel overwhelming. See page 189 for a list of hotlines to find help and information.

A book about sexual trauma has a high likelihood of evoking unsettling emotions, memories, thoughts, or sensations. Any page in this book, even those with more soothing content, can potentially trigger a survivor of sexual assault. In an attempt to give readers more control, I've highlighted pages with safer content using a visual cue (🌱)—essentially, a *reverse* trigger warning. These pages contain little or no material that describes my history. Many of the safer pages focus on self-care. Additionally, on the title page of the core chapters, you'll find a list of the pages within that are "least" triggering. This way, when you have your own dark days, you can explore a topic without needing to wade through my darker material as well.

Some of my terminology, descriptions, and approaches may not resonate with you and your experiences. It is important as a survivor to embrace what feels in alignment with your needs and to pass by what feels unhelpful. I wish you continued healing that comes with as much peace, comfort, and ease as possible. I honor the wisdom within you to create your own healing journey as you read about mine.

Womb

Looking Within

Feel like you need to avoid
possible triggers today?

Skip to pages 19-22

Womb

Emotions hid deep within me for many years. I see *Womb* as the storehouse for those forgotten emotions. A place of pain but also of richness and fertility. The lava of life erupts out of me as a I heal. And I painted its volcanic core.

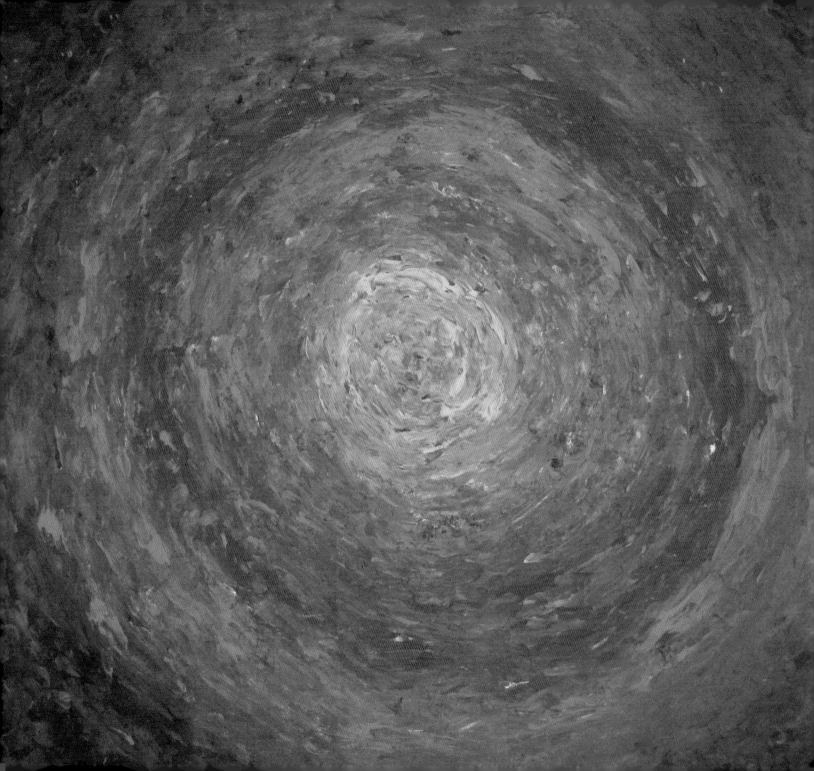

Ruminating

I rented a little house out in the country for a couple of years. I needed a place to be in nature, to lie on the ground, to express strong emotions, to journal, and to paint. Cows grazed nearby. I enjoyed having them close, yet they weren't really "my" kind of creature. I felt an easy affinity with the great blue herons who fished and nested at the pond. The deer and groundhog and occasional coyote captivated me more than the cows.

One day, I had a cow epiphany, thanks to a comment by my therapist. Their deeply grounded, ruminating spirits matched closely to what I craved from this retreat. I needed to find peaceful ground again. To have space to feel the recurring layers of emotions and thoughts. Chew on them a while, swallow them, spit them up, and chew on them more. My old way of being was to judge the darkness within me so I could avoid feeling and expressing it.

Ruminating is called for sometimes. Cows know it's vital. I had to allow myself to exist as I was—emotionally and mentally—before my inner world could shift.

Listen. Chew. Pay attention. Slowly. Perhaps it'll change.

A Byron Katie quote comes to mind: "I don't let go of my thoughts—I meet them with understanding. Then *they* let go of *me*."

I like to apply this philosophy not just to my thoughts, but to all of my inner experiences, such as emotions and sensations. Meet the darkness with understanding; then it will let go and flow through.

Spiraling Inward

Flooded by emotion—with no clear present-day reason—I hurried to the basement to paint this one. My traumatic past revealed itself in whispers and screams within my body. Anger. Fear. Anxiety. Sadness. I smeared red and then squeezed circles of yellow, soothing blue, and white from their bottles. Spiraling my fingers to the center of the paper, the craziness shifted closer to peacefulness. I was learning how to spiral into myself, to recognize what I was feeling, respond soothingly and respectfully, and then release the emotions with ease.

Cultivating Inner Awareness

The key to my healing has been to cultivate a deeper awareness of my inner life. Childhood trauma resulted in my brain's decreased ability to track my emotions, body sensations, and thoughts. While I was hypervigilant of others, closely monitoring my environment, I lost touch with what I felt and thought. This less-aware version of me couldn't see that I was missing anything in my human experience. As a young adult, though, I sought out yoga and massage therapy. They gave me temporary peace. Gradually, they taught me to relax, go slowly, and pay attention to what happens on the inside.

Inner awareness is a river that flows through all of these techniques. A healing force unto itself, embracing this foundational skill helps you progress through therapies with less risk of crumbling.

Picture inner awareness as a basket. The more strands and strength woven into the bowl, the more it can hold as you work through the contents.

Through inner awareness, I met not only wounds needing healing but also an inner voice, my intuition—the loss of which is possibly the most destructive damage I experienced from sexual abuse. For me, intuition is a blend of feelings, thoughts, and sensations. Inner awareness brings these back so they can unite in harmony and guide me in life and healing.

"Body flowing out of Spirit. Spirit flowing from body."

—RUMI

SURVIVOR'S TOOLBOX

Cultivating Inner Awareness

Inner awareness deepens with practice. As I build my inner awareness, I embody my authentic self. As more attention flows within to balance a culture that pulls us outward, we become more alive and grounded. Life can flow through without pushing us into automatic pilot.

I chose to use the term "inner awareness" instead of "mindfulness" because of the specificity of "inner awareness" for directing attention inward. I sense that the word "mind" within "mindfulness" can focus intention towards the head, even though that's not the broader goal of mindfulness. Inner awareness allows for being present within life without losing touch with the wisdom of our bodies full of emotions, thoughts, and sensations. For me, it's the first step in healing.

Here are some ways to help build a stronger relationship with your inner world.

- Progressive relaxation—slowly contract and relax individual muscles from your head to your feet. Then contract all your muscles at once; then relax.
- Pretend your eyes can see into your body. Notice what you "see."
- Write a description or draw what is in you—colors, shapes, movement, directions, regions of unawareness/nothingness, regions of vitality.
- Study anatomy and physiology to help you visualize what is within you. Touch or use a muscle or bone while studying it in a book or website.

- Move more slowly than usual periodically throughout the day. Feel any ripple effects of slow movements in your body and emotional state.
- Speak and listen to areas of the body. It may feel silly, but your attentive mind can tune into what your body needs, using a conversation as an imaginative tool.
- Try yoga or tai chi or qigong. There are lots of free videos online.
- Meditate with an inward focus, not drifting far from your body or focusing on an external object. If sitting still and silent is too challenging, try a walking meditation where you pay attention to your inner world as you walk. Music can assist with meditation, so try various styles of music at varying volumes. Some prime times for meditating are: just after waking in the morning, after exercising, after a massage, during or after a shower or bath, as part of a transition between activities, during a sleepy afternoon time, and before bed.
- Give yourself a massage using slow, deliberate motions, with space to feel nuances of the responses within your body. Vary the pressure.
- Receive massage from a compassionate and calm friend or massage therapist. Pay attention to the touch and your reaction. Always honor your inner "no" or "stop" if the touch does not feel supportive.
- Write down your emotions, thoughts, and body sensations. Set an alarm for every thirty minutes to stretch and take note of your inner life.
- Look in your eyes in a mirror for several minutes. Notice what flows within you.
- In conversations with others, check in with your body, listening within to not lose awareness as you interact with other people. Subtly moving muscles can help keep awareness alive within you. Point your toes up and down. Rotate your ankles. Breathe slowly and deeply.

OPEN SPACE

Look into your mind, your heart, your body. Write. Scribble. Color. Draw.

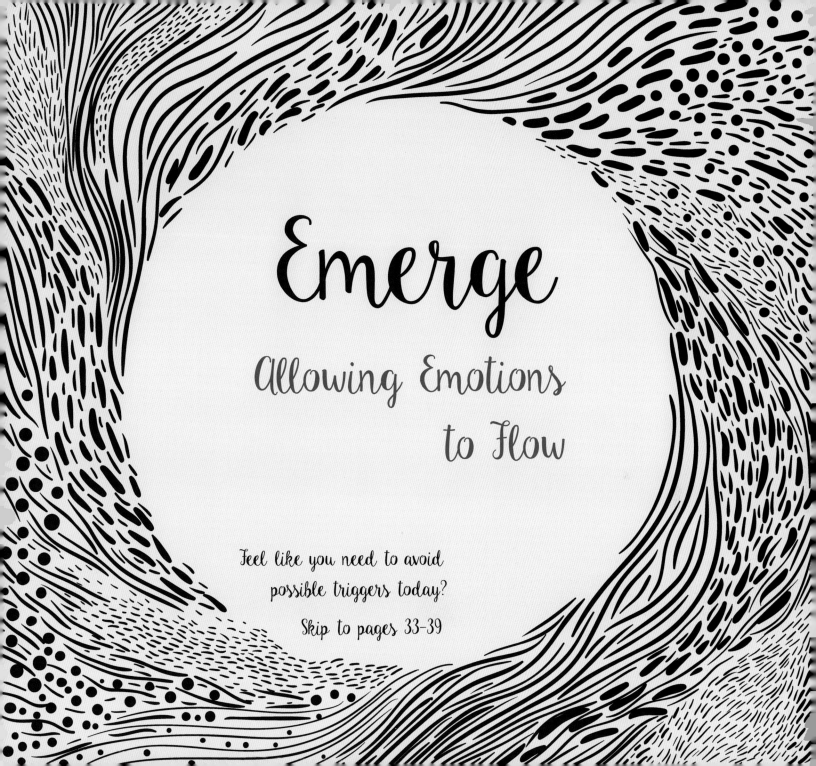

Emerge

Allowing Emotions to Flow

Feel like you need to avoid
possible triggers today?

Skip to pages 33-39

Emerge

This painting has many layers. I smeared white paint over dark paperboard. Then bright colors called to me. The image emerges full of life and a healthy dose of indignation at having been forced to hide so much vitality for so long.

Illuminating Pain

I wish I could simply enjoy the vivid colors of this painting. I can't. Within its depths, there is so much pain, nausea, guilt, shame, darkness, and disgust. I call it *Illuminating Pain* because I've struggled learning to trust these horrid feelings as healing. Yet ... they are. They are the truth of the impacts of abuse. By listening to them and responding with gentle care, I move through them.

A Heart

Even several years after painting it, I still feel *A Heart* reverberate strongly in the center of my chest. Sometimes my reaction to a painting changes over time. This one has yet to shift for me. There is some pain within the core of this image. Some grief. Some loss. Some vibrancy. Some echoes from the past. Some stability within the motion.

It's yoga's pigeon pose . . . or as I eventually come to think of it: weeping pigeon. I breathe into my left hip area, feeling an inner swell of motion nudging against something dense. A jolt of fear runs through me. Part of me says, "Don't go there." I quell my urge to cry. I'm in a classroom of about twenty other yoga students. I rarely let myself cry, even when alone, so there's no way I feel comfortable weeping with acquaintances looking on. Who knows what they'd imagine is going on with me? I don't even know what's going on with me. What I do know is that I'm meeting within myself what I'd heard about in massage school and witnessed in some of my massage clients. Unresolved emotions can be stored in the body. It's not just that relaxation makes space for emotions.

I've been attending regular yoga classes again after giving birth to my son two months ago. I wonder if my hip is letting go of some of the birthing experience—the physical trauma and the emotional roller coaster of the event. Whatever the source, I know it's a place wanting slowness and gentleness. I breathe slowly and try to relax my pelvic muscles more. I'd tensed up when the fear first came through.

Breathing slowly helps. The fear subsides.

The urge to cry dissipates.

Through more yoga practice at home and at classes, I continued to visit this area of potent emotions in my pelvis. Some of it softens with focused breathing. I sense my attention alone helps ease the tension and emotional potency. I'm listening.

I now know what I was meeting within myself. Childhood sexual abuse, long forgotten by the mysterious mechanisms of my protective self, which helped me live with unhealed trauma by sealing it away in my body and mind. My pelvis experienced earthquakes from sexual abuse by a trusted professional as a young adult and then later during pregnancy and childbirth. The rumblings took layers of sealant off the stored memories. My yoga practice was gently removing more of the coverings. I was attentively caring for myself so my full self was feeling safe enough to emerge.

Allowing Emotions to Flow

Coping alone with unhealed trauma taught me to ignore my emotions and bundle them up. Eventually I stopped feeling most of them. As I reconnected to my emotions, I needed to learn how to "be" with my feelings. With the help of therapists, I approached all emotions with less judgment. I realized that for the traumatized parts of myself, the dark, frightening emotions needed to be validated and treated with respect. They were what I hadn't had an opportunity to feel during or after the abuse.

I learned to exist with the feelings, allowing them in whatever form they came. It wasn't easy early on. Emotions tended to gush forcefully. Sometimes I cried for hours. Gradually, though, this necessary catharsis eased. I felt relief by letting emotions run their course without trying to stop or change them. Emotions were both the core of the trauma wounds and the healing balm. Over time, the frequencies and life cycles of my emotions have decreased dramatically. I've purged much of the emotional backlog. Now I celebrate times when my present-day life evokes an emotion that comes and goes naturally within a few minutes.

The concept of forgiveness has been problematic for my emotional healing. When thinking about forgiveness, I usually feel pressure to hurry up and get over my pain. It pushes me back toward emotional suppression and judgment, especially when other people suggest that I need to forgive in order to heal. There is no shame in taking *your* time to heal, regardless of length. I believe forgiveness arises organically and deepens as wounds are healed. When an abuser takes responsibility and makes emotional and financial amends, forgiveness may arise more easily within a victim. But for others, this will not be the case, nor should forgiveness be expected.

Some spiritual traditions teach of detaching from emotions. I came to understand that this approach doesn't work well for me. It resembles dissociation too closely. I've learned to witness my feelings without detaching from them or avoiding them. During this time of reclaiming and honoring authentic feelings, I rarely find a benefit in reframing or positive thinking as a way to exit an emotion. As trauma survivors, indeed as human beings, we need to take part in our emotions by engaging lovingly and feeling them in our bodies.

For me, emotional freedom comes from flowing emotions.

CREATIVE SELF-CARE FOR ALLOWING EMOTIONS TO FLOW

When I feel stuck or avoidant or overwhelmed by emotions, I rely on a variety of self-care techniques.

- **Resting**—I give myself time and space to just feel.
- **Talking**—Often I seek out a compassionate friend or therapist to listen to what is arising within me.
- **Painting**—See Survivor's Toolbox for Expressive Painting with Inner Awareness on page 36.
- **"Rememberings and Celebrations: Loving Reminders of the Great Mother's Voice"**—These affirmation cards by Robyn Posin encourage a nurturing voice inside. I read, re-read, and absorb the messages on the cards so they become part of how I relate to my emotional world.
- **Swimming in flowing water**—Water teaches me how to let life and emotions flow.
- **Butterfly hug**—By crossing arms in front of my chest, I tap first on one shoulder and then on the other. This gets the left and right brain hemispheres communicating. Uncomfortable emotions and sensations seem to drain out of me. It works on chest, hips, and legs, as well as shoulders. This is most effective when I can turn my attention softly inward. This exercise comes from Eye Movement Desensitization and Reprocessing (EMDR) therapy, discussed in more detail on page 181.
- **Journaling**—Writing down descriptions of how I'm feeling often helps me edge closer to the heart of an emotion. It's validation to wounded parts within me that I am listening now.

- **Acupressure self-care routines**—*Acupressure for Emotional Healing* by Michael Reed Gach and Beth Ann Henning outlines many routines to tend various emotions and conditions, including anxiety, sexual abuse, PTSD, and chronic fatigue.
- **Forest bathing**—The Japanese have a term, *shinrin-yoku,* that translates as "forest bathing." The concept resonates deeply with me, as I find much relief, comfort, and invigoration when I spend time in the woods.
- **Aromatherapy**—I choose essential oils based on what I'm drawn to and how I feel after smelling the oil. Eucalyptus, frankincense, rosemary, cedarwood, and clary sage work well for a variety of my symptoms. A combination of frankincense, marjoram, and grapefruit works well for my anxiety patterns. I add them to salt baths or to a small necklace pendant that can hold a couple drops. Essential oil diffusers provide a roomful of scent.
- **Salt bath**—I add a half to one cup of sea salt to the bath for a five- to twenty-minute soak. Cleansing and refreshing, remnants of heavy emotions wash away. I add herbs and flowers for aroma and whimsy. I love putting in long rosemary sprigs from my garden.

SURVIVOR'S TOOLBOX

Painting toward Wholeness:

Expressive Painting with Inner Awareness

Try abstract painting with your hands (no brushes) to help move through emotions and sensations. The "abstract" intention helps me to quiet my inner critic by saying, "It's not supposed to look like anything." Whatever swirls or glops or patterns emerge is just right. If you are hesitant to try painting on your own, find an art therapist to help you explore creatively healing.

You will need:

- Large paper or paperboard cut from a cereal box
- Acrylic paint (cheap brands work fine!)
- Latex gloves in your size
- Newspaper
- Paper towels or rags in case of spills

You may need:

- A friend to sit near you or to be reachable by phone
- Your therapist's phone number
- Tissues to catch the tears

1. Cover a table or floor with newspaper. Or use an old table you want to dedicate to painting—my painting table is a work of abstract art itself.
2. Place your paper or paperboard on the newspaper. If using a cereal box, use the brown inner surface.
3. Put on latex gloves unless you're using nontoxic paints.
4. If you like, turn on music that relaxes you or suits your mood.
5. Sit for a few minutes and turn inward. Listen and feel the details of what is stirring within you.
6. Set an intention if one comes to mind. For example: "I set the intention for releasing nausea from my stomach as well as moving this anger through and out of me."
7. Choose whatever color or colors you feel drawn to. Squirt or drip the color onto your paper. If you like, make a pattern or shape as you do so. Feel free to use multiple colors for this step.
8. Using flat palms, fingertips, and/or sides of hand, spread, swirl, make lines, create patterns, etc. in the paint. Notice your feelings and sensations as you do this. Close your eyes if you find yourself judging the painting.
9. Add more paint or different colors. Try painting motions that flow toward the center. Try outward motions. Try clockwise versus counterclockwise motions. Notice how you feel as you vary how your fingers, hands, arms, and body are moving. Repeat those motions that feel supportive. Breathe. Cry. Yell. Sing. Hum. Stomp your feet— whatever helps. If it feels right, imagine any uncomfortable sensations exiting your body through your hands into the paint or down into the earth. Stop if the emotions get too intense, if you feel done, if the emotions have resolved, or if you find a visual stopping place in your painting that you want to honor.
10. Take off the latex gloves, and then hold your palms above the painting. Imagine all residual feelings flowing out of you into the painting. I like to think paintings enjoy being fed this way.

$\longrightarrow$

11. As they dry, paintings can stick to newspaper if the paint went over the edges, so shift it to a dry area of newspaper or a washable, dry surface. Hanging them also works if the paint doesn't drip.
12. Take some time to sit and notice your inner world. Journal or take a bath or do stretches or yoga.

If it feels good to you, display the dry painting where you can have time alone to experience the work when you wish. I believe that a painting can subtly communicate with the creator and others. Let the paintings play a role in your healing. Sometimes, a painting may hold too much triggering pain, so it's okay to tuck it away in a closet or under a bed for a while. Or it may be healing to tear up or burn a painting. Take photos of it as another way to witness what has left you and now resides in the painting. Or take the painting to therapy as a way to access the feelings.

OPEN SPACE

Look into your mind, your heart, your body. Write. Scribble. Color. Draw.

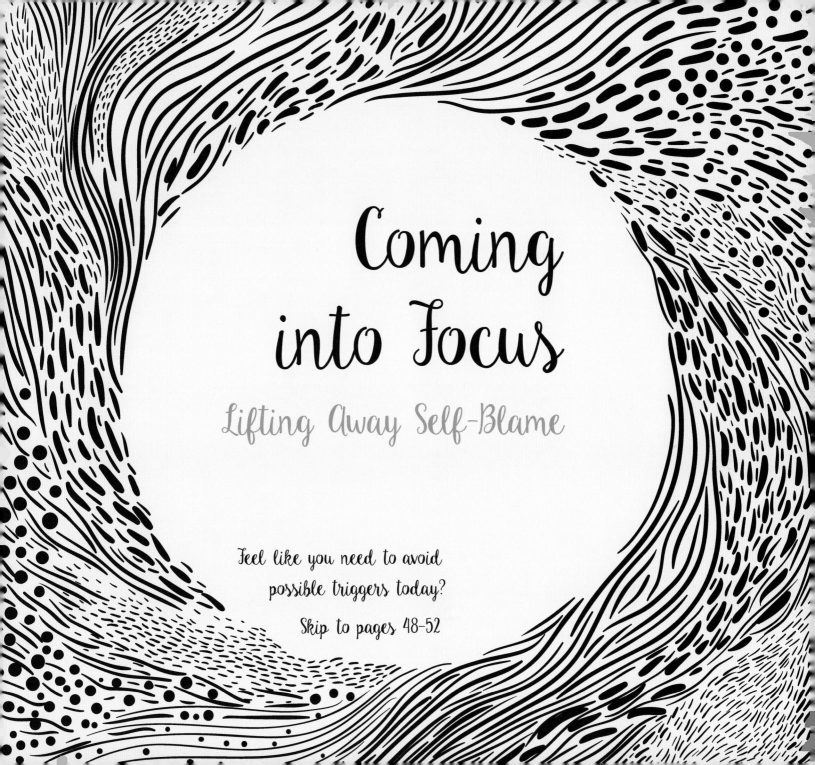

Coming into Focus

Lifting Away Self-Blame

Feel like you need to avoid
possible triggers today?

Skip to pages 48-52

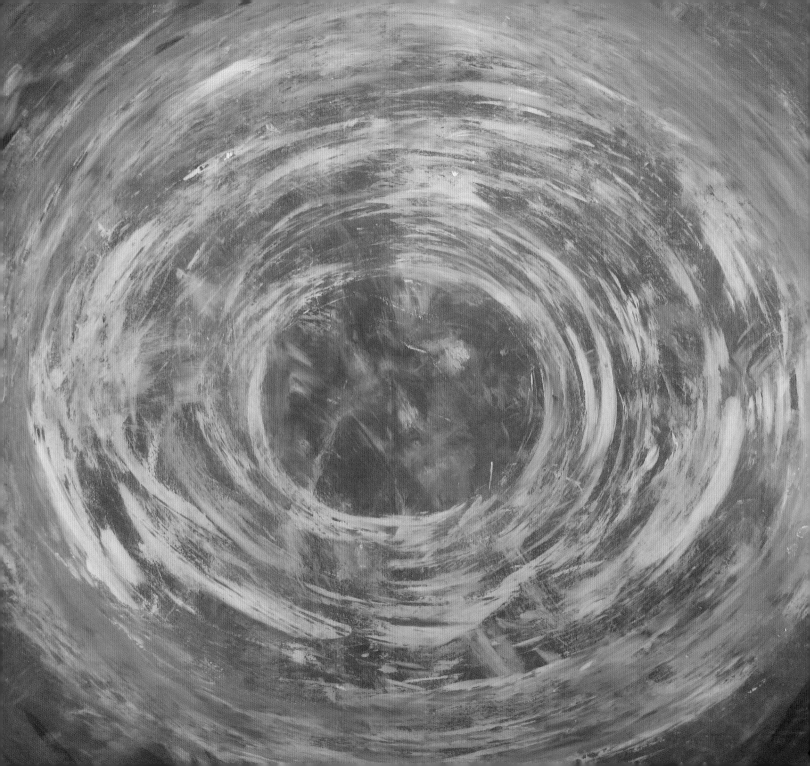

Coming into Focus

I painted *Coming into Focus* around the same time as *Out Rage* (page 122). They hold similar imprints, as clarity was starting to seep into my brain and body. Fiery emotions cleared the way for truths of the past and a vision for my future. None of what I had endured was my fault. It was dizzying for me to try to balance between the two worlds—a false world created by abusers that clouded my vision and a true world of innocence violated. Dismay and rage dominated as I struggled to stay in my newly discovered authenticity. Yet self-blame seemed true at the time, even though it wasn't. I held each moment with a surprised respect. I didn't know how long I'd keep feeling like my feelings were valid, that I was not crazy and not to blame for the abuse. *Coming into Focus* emerged as a symbol of immense hope for me. Later, the balances would shift so the majority of my days would be filled with times of feeling clear, strong, and whole rather than rattled, drained, and broken.

I wanted to access my own power to create my life.

Small Me

There were moments, hours, and days when I felt overwhelmed by doubt, by thinking no one would believe me. I had no proof. I scribbled on construction paper with crayons. The activity facilitated my expression of the "small me" who was violated. Raw pain mixed with a fear that I must be crazy to feel so messed up. Maybe I was just too sensitive? Maybe I was just confused? Would anyone believe me if I spoke of it? Eventually, I read about sexual abuse and how common it is for the victim to get caught in patterns of self-doubt and self-blame. I began to understand that my guilt and doubt weren't accurate. When these emotions weighed me down, I'd nurture myself with phrases like "I believe you," "It wasn't your fault," and "Yes, you were abused." The thick, sticky burden eased. My body felt lighter and less shaky with each moment I recognized and shifted out of these thoughts and emotions. One of the most liberating perspectives was that these heavy thoughts and emotions were not truly me. They belonged to abusers and society's conditioning. They were not the truth. I could scrub them off, paint them away, stomp them into dust, and firmly say no to them.

I awaken this morning lying on my back, a body position that usually triggers me. I wait for the buzzing anxiety to appear. It doesn't. I'm relieved. But the heavy lead is there. A frozen anvil is in my chest and gut, keeping me on my back against my will. I say to myself, "Get up." "Roll over." But the lead holds me in place. After a minute or two, I manage to push through it and get out of bed. I'm still tired but wary of lying down again. I decide to gather pillows around me and lie down on my belly, holding my heart and upper chest where the panic is starting to make its fluttery entrance. I'd hoped to avoid that. I breathe slowly and speak soothing words to myself, to my imaginings of myself at age four or five, the little one who in the last six months has been telling me about really scary stuff that a man did to her. I'm surprised when the soothing doesn't work.

Then thoughts come into my head about what happened later in my life. Tears and relief come as I turn my soothing attention to the young woman within me. It reminds me that in many ways I'm so hard on her, when she really deserves the same openness and comfort I give to the violated four-year-old.

The young woman didn't have a clue about what was happening. She trusted him. I fold inward with the pain. She's confused and wants to call out for help. I imagine going to her. She wants to collapse into a puddle in the corner of the room and cry. But she doesn't. She's had decades of practice doubting herself and holding in her feelings. Shaking and spinning, she wonders why the clothes that were so comfortable two hours before have somehow changed. The jean shorts feel abrasive and heavy. The red shirt with an elaborate Japanese landscape is too scratchy and hot. I loved that shirt. I gave it to Goodwill this year. I'd kept thinking I'd be strong enough someday to wear it again so I kept it for a long time. Eventually, I stopped struggling to "get over it" and "move on." I'm embracing the depth of the wounds. If I couldn't willfully rid myself of the emotional pain, at least I could get rid of the shirt. So now someone else is enjoying wearing the crane flying over the Japanese garden.

I remember to pay attention to the woman, not the clothes. I tell her, "I'm so sorry he did that to you." I say, "It's not your fault." "He had no right." I put my arms around her, and she softens and weeps. But she does not believe my words. She feels certain that it's her fault. She must have given him the idea it was what she wanted. I hold her. Being with her is all I can do. Logic won't sink in right now.

I'm back in the present moment, on my bed, on my belly, holding my heart and rocking slightly. The tears continue to flow for a few minutes, washing the panic out of my chest. I get up and blow my nose. I hear my son moving in his room. My crying might have awakened him. I hear him padding softly toward my room. I blow my nose again and put on a smile, grateful that I do feel joy behind the smile . . . it'll be a genuine smile for him. I hug him and say, "Happy Birthday! You're five!"

Disappearing Self-Blame

Cleansing my psyche of self-blame was the first big phase of healing for me. I hadn't received solid validation from a number of people I'd sought out for help, and this piled on more self-doubt. Self-blame is part of most survivors' experiences. I'd always thought that blaming yourself for abuse was unfair, yet I'd fallen into the same trap. Self-blame suggested to me that the only person I needed to be angry with was myself. It also is a way to deny that a "true" violation occurred. The fight-or-flight response isn't the only option hardwired in us; the "freeze" reaction is common when we feel threatened. That knowledge was a huge turning point for my recovery. Doubting victims, in part, comes from not understanding these neurological responses to traumatic events.[1]

I recognized self-blame more clearly when it descended like a suffocating fog on my mind. I started writing down the blaming statements flowing through my head and from people around me. I "asked for it." I'm "just confused." I'm "crazy." I "let it happen." I recorded how I felt inside when I heard these inner and outer messages. I began to feel the connection between body symptoms and self-blame. As I cleared my mind of doubt and blame, fatigue, depression, and anxiety faded. My emotions of sadness and anger, more directly related to being violated, flowed with more clarity. I could then fully embrace trauma healing.

Thankfully, social media and victim advocacy groups are raising awareness of the many manifestations of our rape culture, including overt and subtle blaming and doubting of victims. This silences victims and trains them to blame themselves when abused.

Self-blame still creeps into me occasionally. It holds less potency, though. I recognize it quickly and speak to myself in understanding and clarifying ways. *I have not done anything wrong. I put my trust in abusers and was victimized. I did not bring this on myself. It's natural for a person's body and mind to freeze during traumatic events. I did not ask for this as some life lesson for spiritual growth. I did not create this.*

---

1   James Hopper, "Why many rape victims don't fight or yell," *The Washington Post,* June 23, 2015, http://www.washington post.com/news/grade-point/wp/2015/06/23/why-many-rape-victims-dont-fight-or-yell/?postshare=1291435091428544.

I have doubts about speaking up and writing openly because it's exhausting to sort through the opinions of those who blame. Or even to meet the silence of those just thinking rather than expressing those attitudes.

I am compelled more strongly, though, by a clear inner sense that openness is exactly what's needed to transform these harmful messages into healing messages.

CREATIVE SELF-CARE FOR SELF-BLAME

To tend feelings of self-blame and self-doubt, I usually choose cathartic expressions and cleansing self-care techniques like these below.

- **Journaling**—I allow myself to write out the dark, vicious thoughts. Then I write compassionate responses to them.
- **Self-talk/affirmations**—I "re-parent" the self-blaming, wounded parts of myself.

  I've done nothing wrong.
  This is not my fault.
  The abuser chose to abuse.
  It's okay to let these feelings go.

- **Reading the book *Resurrection After Rape***—With contributions by many survivors, Matt Atkinson's book, especially the section on identifying stuck points, assisted me in shaking free from self-blame. The concepts explored apply to healing from all types of sexual violation, not just from rape.
- **Butterfly hug**—By crossing arms in front of my chest, I tap first on one shoulder and then on the other. This gets the left and right brain hemispheres communicating. Uncomfortable emotions and sensations seem to drain out of me. It works on chest, hips, and legs, as well as shoulders. This is most effective when I can turn my attention softly inward. This exercise comes from Eye Movement Desensitization and Reprocessing (EMDR) therapy, discussed in more detail on page 181.
- **Alternate nostril breathing**—A practice from yoga traditions. I inhale through left nostril while holding the right nostril closed. Then I exhale through the right while my left nostril is closed. Next, I inhale through my right nostril while the left nostril remains closed. Finally, I exhale through the left while the right is closed. I repeat the

cycle several times. This practice helps clear my foggy brain, which often accompanies self-blaming and self-doubting thoughts.

- **Lying on the ground**—I rest on a blanket or directly on the ground. Surrendering, tummy-side down, into the earth is a very potent self-care technique for me.
- **Salt bath**—I add a half to one cup of sea salt to the bath for a five- to twenty-minute soak. I imagine the heavy, painful self-blame leaving my body and dissolving into the water.
- **Screaming/venting out sounds**—Encouraging myself to get angry is a powerful way to break out of self-blame mode. It can feel right to simply let anger out in general. Other times I benefit from imagining I'm directing the anger and blame toward the abuser.
- **Avoiding certain people**—Understanding that other people's moods and even thoughts can impact me was a major turning point in my healing. When someone says something that is even vaguely victim-blaming, I then know to avoid that person, if possible, when I am feeling vulnerable.

OPEN SPACE

Look into your mind, your heart, your body. Write. Scribble. Color. Draw.

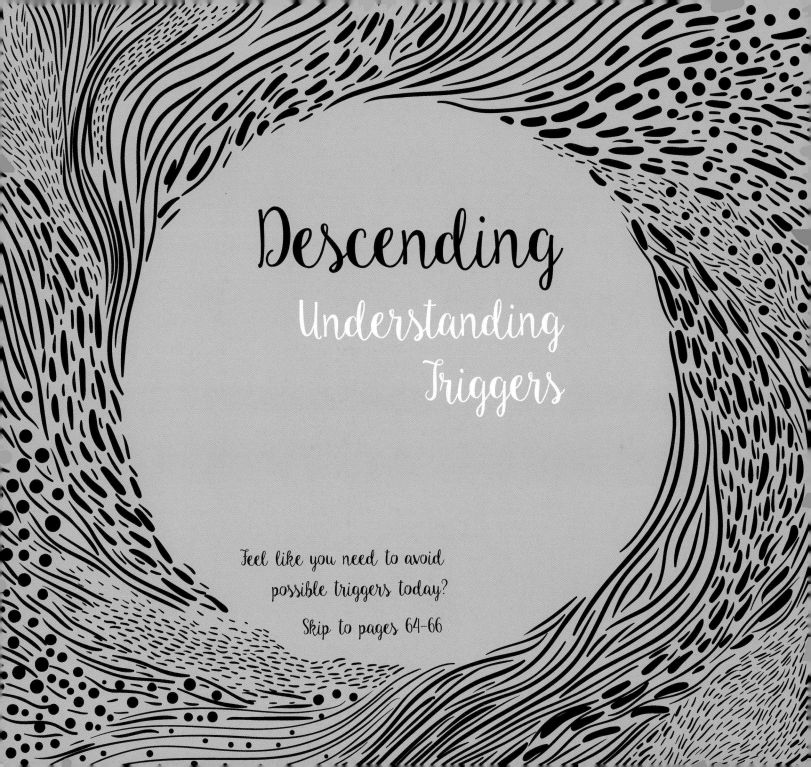

Descending

Understanding Triggers

Feel like you need to avoid
possible triggers today?

Skip to pages 64-66

Descending

Descending depicts the caverns within me. For several years, when something reminded me of the sexual violations, I fell into these places of dark, uncomfortable feelings. The past pain presented itself to be listened to and healed. I crawled through gnarly, hard feelings, through intense heat and chills, through pain filling my body with aches, pinches, and surges.

It was a hell.

Somehow glimmers of heaven and peace stayed alive within me. They were tiny, fleeting awarenesses, yet they may have been the only reasons I never considered suicide[2], which is so commonly considered by sexual abuse victims.[3] This is one of the few paintings for which I used a paintbrush. It was one of my son's brushes, hardened with paint that hadn't been washed off. Like a knife, the dried edge carved into the paint to create these caverns.

---

2   If you or someone you know is thinking about suicide, seek professional help or call 1-800-273-TALK (8255) for the National Suicide Prevention Lifeline.

3   Kilpatrick, D. 2000. *The mental health impact of rape.* Charleston, SC: Medical University of South Carolina.

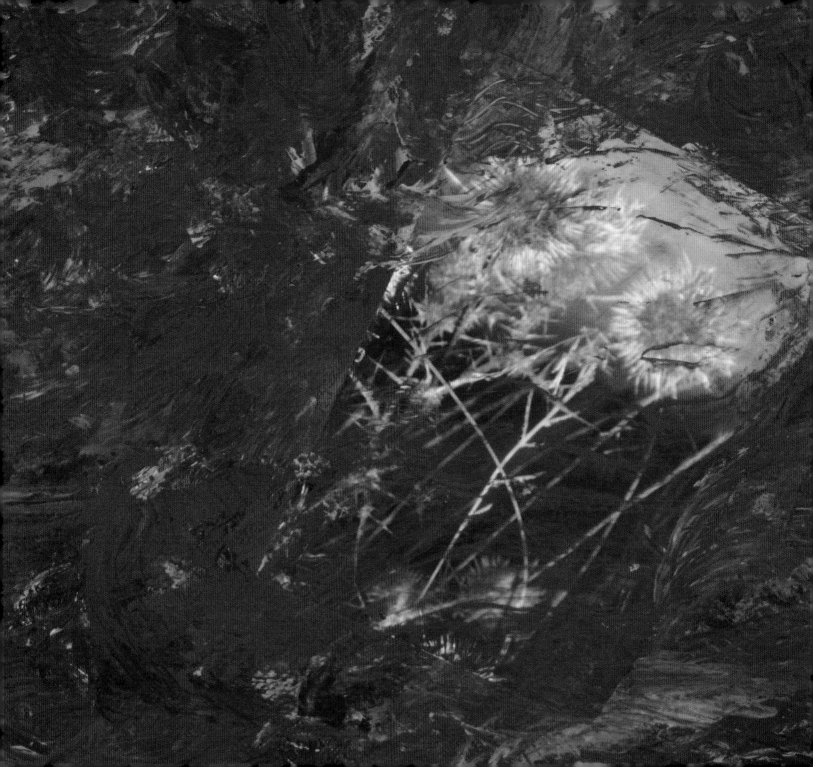

Grieving

Intense physical pain and weeping accompanied the creation of this painting. I'd framed many of my photographs yet hadn't framed the one embedded in *Grieving*. The camera flash starkly illuminates winter weeds at sunset. I'd taken the photo a couple of years before, near where I was abused as a child, and before I had clear mental memories of the trauma. But my body had already begun grieving before my mind.

Mind struggling with body. Mind resisting because it didn't understand why my body was so filled with anxiety from being so close to where abuse had happened. I can still feel the dense knot in my stomach. This photo symbolizes the strange progression of grief communication between body, mind, and soul. As I wept and painted, the photo seemed to belong in the grieving colors. I stuck it into the wet paint and continued to paint for while. Several times, I covered it with paint and then uncovered it, as though trying to decide if the past needed a shallow or deep grave. I feel relief by giving the photo a home within the painting.

Today I'm feeling a little spacey. There's some dread in me. I wonder if this will turn out to be a not-so-good day. I use the brain/body balancing routine called the "Cortices Technique" from BodyTalk.[4] I feel a little better for a while, but one hour later, I am feeling increasingly irritable and tired. The auditory trigger of other people chewing is especially aggravating during lunchtime. I want to yell and run away. My pelvis feels unstable, as though my bones are too loosely connected. I lie down and tell myself soothing phrases like "I'm here with you" and "It's okay to feel this way." I press my feet into my bed's footboard, alternating left with right. I fall asleep for a few minutes while I hear my son watching TV downstairs. We go grocery shopping before dinner. When we return, I feel very spacey. I am buzzing with anxiety surrounding me but not deep within me. I sit on the kitchen floor with my back to the wall and feet flat on the floor, knees close to my chest. I cry for a minute. I grab a pen and paper and feel a strong, downward flowing, comforting sensation as I write this out and imagine the four-year-old me holding the pen and helping from within. She seems to be the one needing to talk right now and to have me acknowledge what she's feeling. The buzzing anxious feelings are now concentrated sensations around the top, back, and sides of my head. It's a swirling, oblong halo. What is swirling? A memory? It seems like this is the dread of sensing the abuser approaching me. I decide to practice the breath of fire technique from yoga, in and out quickly through my nose. It's a way to build up fiery strength of the sort I would have needed had it been safe for me to get furious at my abuser and tell him to stop. The swirling, buzzing feelings stop as I let myself get angry. They seem to crumble off of my head and skin. I feel some relief but still feel spacey. I do deep pressure dragging of my lower legs and arms on my yoga mat to help make me feel more solid and steady. I take my blanket outside and rest on the ground for thirty minutes. I feel much better.

---

4   See page 184 for more information.

Clarifying Triggers

After lifting away self-blame, I started reading more about healing from trauma and how victims can be "triggered" by present day experiences. When triggered, survivors may be flooded by emotions, or they may dissociate from their feelings. I started paying attention to when I felt shifts in my mood, body tension, and physical sensations. I identified what might be reminding my mind and body of the abuse. Triggers often pulled me into emotional modes that mirrored how I felt during and after sexual abuse. I am catapulted into what I describe as healing episodes, like the one on the previous page.

For a long while, I didn't like the term "trigger." It wasn't part of my previous vocabulary except when talking about guns. A few people I'd sought help from had used it dismissively about parts of my experience: "Oh, that was a just a trigger." It minimized the pain inflicted by abuse I experienced as an adult. They seemed to suggest that I was confused about the more recent experience and that the only traumas that had impacted me were the ones that happened in childhood.

Eventually, after reading more about trauma healing, I came to appreciate the term for how it describes present-day experiences that automatically and quickly reawaken patterns of emotions, thoughts, sensations, and other forms of memories. In my view, there are two categories of trauma triggers: lowercase-T triggers and capital-T Triggers. The former are triggers that are harmless in the present day but remind me (or my body) of past abuse. Capital-T Triggers are current, abusive experiences that are emotionally or physically unsafe for me now and also remind me of past abuse. Both types can bring about deeply unsettled feelings. My brain is attempting to keep me safe by noticing experiences similar to ones when I was hurt. This can be helpful when it's a Trigger and yet exhaustingly unhelpful when it's a trigger.

Keeping track of both kinds of triggers and learning their nuances helps me navigate them. This level of comfort and loving awareness eases the severity of triggered responses. With an early-alert system, I can recognize when my brain switches into trauma patterns and respond with intentional self-care. Sometimes avoidance of triggers is necessary, especially on days when I already feel too emotionally vulnerable or have frazzled nerves.

When I tried to grit my way through avoidable triggers, I often felt like it pushed me backwards in healing. The new protective coverings over my raw nerves were scraped off. By allowing myself to steer clear of as many triggers as possible for a couple of years, my nervous system could heal faster.

The fact that I have a sensory processing disorder, as well as PTSD, complicates my world of triggers. Sensory experiences may ignite trauma patterns. To help make sense of it all, I made a categorized list of my triggering experiences. Some of these relate to sensations or experiences during abuse. Some are more indirect, triggering trauma patterns by irritating a nervous system already damaged by abuse. As I've been healing, the power of some triggers has waned. Some are no longer triggers. Some remain intensely disturbing.

Auditory Triggers: being yelled at, loud people and places, sound of people chewing, sound of utensils on dishes.

Tactile Triggers: being touched directly on my skin, touching someone's skin, heavy jeans, silks, most unnatural fabrics, strong wind, smooth sheets, tight clothes, tight bras, dresses, swimming/floating in water, being hit, physically aggressive sports.

Setting Triggers: being near the locations where the abuse happened, in a bedroom, on a bed, crowded places, curtains closed all the way, closed interior doors.

Body Position Triggers: reclining, lying flat on my back.

Verbal Triggers: the word "panties," subtle or overt victim-blaming comments, being blamed without understanding why I'm being blamed.

Sexual & Body Triggers: people looking at my body, being around men (the gender of my abusers), anyone complimenting or judging my physical appearance, sexual innuendos and jokes, penises and phallic objects, movies or stories with sexual assaults or intimate relationships between people with a large age or power differential, sexual arousal, sexual intercourse, masturbation, being naked even when alone, nudity.

Physiological Triggers: elevated heart rate, elevated heart rate in others, rapid breathing in others, muscle soreness.

When I feel overwhelmed, I look through my list of triggers to identify anything that might have happened recently to throw me off balance. Then I respond soothingly, in an understanding and less judgmental/annoyed/frustrated way.

CREATIVE SELF-CARE FOR TRIGGERS

Being triggered calls for self-care. Here is a sampling of self-care choices I find helpful to ease out of a traumatized state. The entire self-care arsenal, found in the "Building a Foundation of Creative Self-Care" chapter (page 155), is useful for triggers.

- **Self-talk/affirmations**—Often the first tool I try, self-talk can bring clarity and peace back to the part of me that feels triggered, much like a compassionate parent speaking to a frightened child. Self-talk boosts the soothing power of other self-care techniques.

  Let's take a deep breath.
  This reminds me of the abuse, but this isn't the abuse.
  Right now I am safe.
  This feels like too much for now, so let's go home.

- **Lying on the ground**—I rest facedown on a blanket and surrender my weight to the earth. I allow the triggered feelings to flow out of me into the ground.
- **Holding rocks or placing them under my feet**—Similar to the practice of holding a worry stone, I find comfort in holding rocks. Feeling their solidity and stability acts as a counterbalance to unrest.
- **Butterfly hug**—By crossing arms in front of my chest, I tap first on one shoulder and then on the other. This gets the left and right brain hemispheres communicating. Uncomfortable emotions and sensations seem to drain out of me. It works on chest, hips, and legs, as well as shoulders. This is most effective when I can turn my attention softly inward. This exercise comes from Eye Movement Desensitization and Reprocessing (EMDR) therapy, discussed in more detail on page 181.

- **Journaling**—Writing about where a trigger has taken me emotionally, mentally, and physically can help me pull out of a triggered state. Journaling can reveal nuances of the meaning and power of a trigger.
- **Dancing**—To clear out what's rattling inside me, I benefit from putting on some music and allowing my body to flow with the sounds and my emotions.
- **Crying/screaming/venting out any sounds**—I say what I need to say.
- **Salt bath**—I add a half to one cup sea salt (coarse or fine) to the bath for a five- to twenty-minute soak. Very cleansing. This is a good way to end a self-care routine.
- **Resting**
- **Aromatherapy**—I choose essential oils based on what I'm drawn to and how I feel after smelling the oil. Eucalyptus, frankincense, rosemary, cedarwood, and clary sage work well for a variety of my symptoms. A combination of frankincense, marjoram, and grapefruit works well for my anxiety patterns.

OPEN SPACE

Look into your mind, your heart, your body. Write. Scribble. Color. Draw.

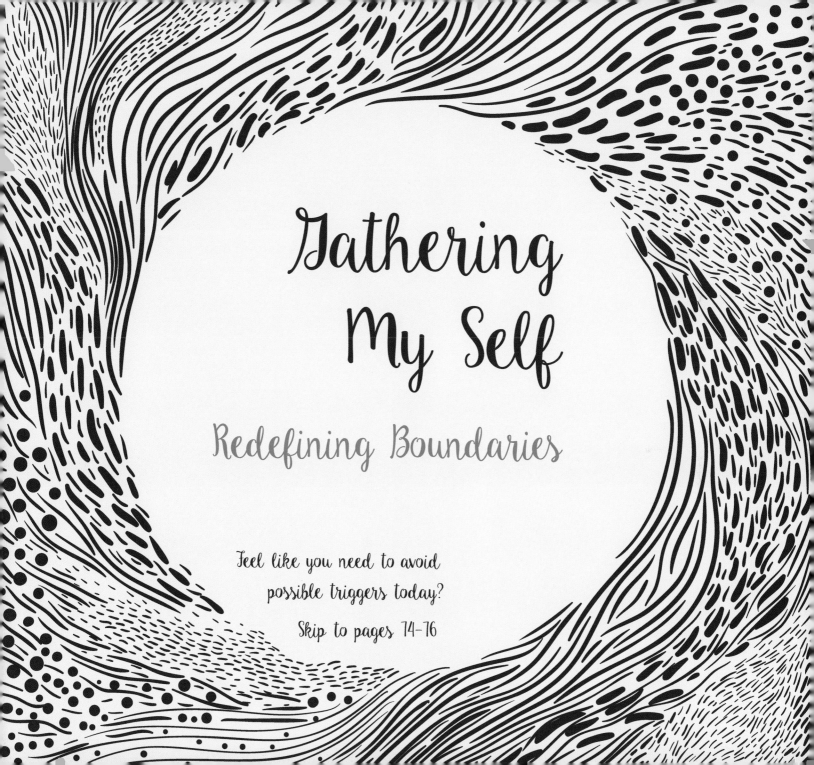

Gathering My Self

Redefining Boundaries

Feel like you need to avoid
possible triggers today?

Skip to pages 74-76

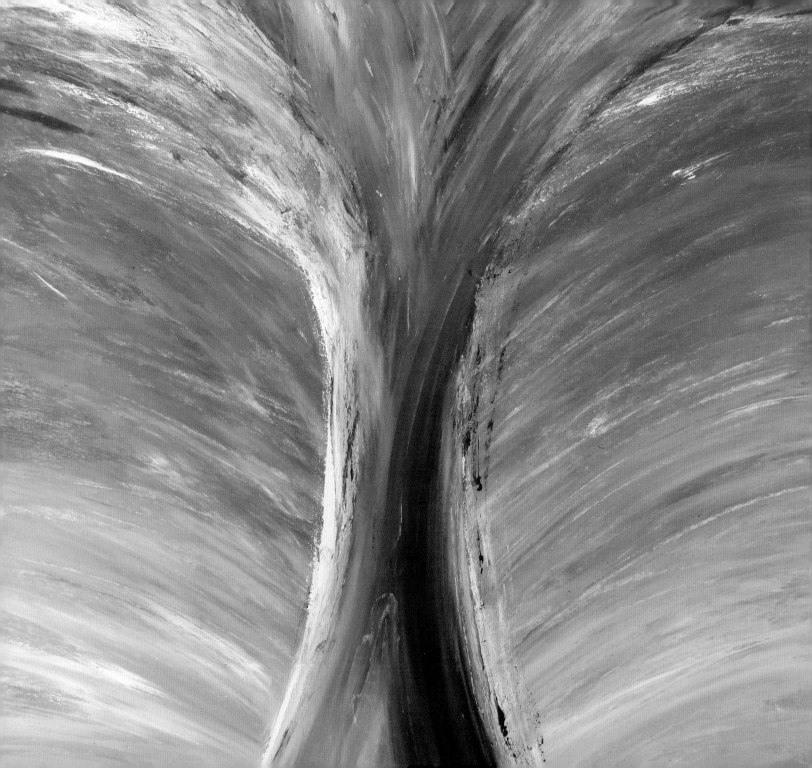

Me, a Tree . . . Self-Portrait on a Good Day

Trees inspire me. They're powerfully rooted. They harness energy from the earth, air, and sun. I see in *Me, a Tree* how important it's been to learn to harness energy and keep it within me by creating durable edges where in the past only holes existed. Violation shredded my boundaries, letting me leak out and letting others enter in. A professional mentor took advantage of pathways created by childhood sexual and emotional abuse. I didn't have a clear awareness of what was me, what wasn't, and what I felt. I'd adapted to looking outside myself to gauge the safety of my surroundings. I lost touch with myself.

Me, a Tree is a good-day portrait because of the solid edges as it rises up to be expressive. On bad days, I'd be painted as droopy, undefined, hazy. It's those days that I feel PTSD symptoms most acutely: hypersensitivity to sounds and touch, superficial full-body pain, cloudy thinking, general uneasiness and anxiety, avoiding men, and avoiding people experiencing strong emotions. I'm grateful these bad days appear less frequently now. *Me, a Tree* is a prayer for holding steady and solid within myself.

People

Life force dances through us. *People* speaks of the complexities of connecting with others. I feel small quivers of fear as I look at *People*. I've struggled to trust. I've struggled to not blend with others, to hold myself distinct and not morph to fit the needs of another person. This is related to my ongoing work in healing the holes from violation. Yet I hold a vision of being at peace as I engage with others. There can be fluidity, grace, and beauty in connecting with others in the dance of life.

Redefining Boundaries

I am not a soccer field or a basketball court. That's what it sounded like though when therapists said that what I'd experienced was a "boundary violation" and leave the description at that. While for some people this phrase may feel supportive, for me it sounded empty, as though an abuser had impacted only the outer periphery of my being. It didn't convey an understanding of the real damage being done. The frequent use of "boundaries" in psychology and its use within so many non-trauma topics has washed out the meaning and made the impact less potent. I learned to ask therapists to replace or elaborate on the word using more descriptive terms. It felt more validating to hear that these were invasive attacks on the core of my body and soul. Sexual violations of all kinds do damage that can be overwhelming and shocking. Not that the abuser deserved a penalty card in soccer. Not that he made some unethical misstep out of bounds and broke a set of rules, rather than me.

I came to see value in the concept of boundaries. Protective zones of my existence had been shredded, burned, and decimated. Nothing kept out the world. Crowds, the grocery store, other people's emotions all flattened me for a long while—and still do on occasion. Many victims have been told in a judgmental way that they have "poor" boundaries. Imagine if a burn victim were chastised for not having skin capable of functioning in a healthy way in the world. "Poor" may be a *poor* choice of words.

Challenges with emotional and relational boundaries can most helpfully be described as an understandable symptom of sexual abuse and not the victim's fault. I suffered a damaging invasion that dissolved my body/mind/nervous system's ability to feel comfortable inside myself. It also clouded my awareness of my feelings and intuition while I was being overwhelmed with tending other people's feelings and needs rather than my own. It takes time to learn to say a healthy "no" when it's been deeply ingrained that it is unsafe to do so. Addressing trauma in healing ways is organically rebuilding my boundaries, boundary awareness, and comfort with setting boundaries in relationships.

CREATIVE SELF-CARE FOR STRENGTHENING BOUNDARIES

Emotional, physical/sensory, and mental boundaries can all be strengthened through a variety of self-care techniques.

- **Journaling**—By refining how I think and feel about my inner and outer lives, I can explore the solid "lines" of who I am.
- **Cultivating inner awareness**—See Survivor's Toolbox on page 20. When I am more aware of what is happening inside me, I can more easily detect shifts within me to discern when others feel invasive.
- **Saying no or yes in congruence with my authentic promptings**—This is a verbal way of creating boundaries and shifting out anything that needs to be cleansed. "No, you don't get to dump on me," and "Yes, I have the right to decide what works for me."
- **Rebuilding boundaries through the body**—See Survivor's Toolbox on page 88.
- **Colored light meditation**—Using my imagination, I envision myself being filled and surrounded by colors that appeal in the moment. I imagine the edges of the light field to be strong yet flexible, with no holes or thin sections.
- **Breath of fire**—A yogic breathing technique in which the abdomen, especially near the diaphragm, is rapidly pulled inward toward the spine while exhaling quickly through the nose. The inhalations naturally follow the exhalations. Rapid repetition for a minute leaves me feeling more energized and free from feeling invaded. To keep from feeling ungrounded, I envision the energy flowing inward and downward.
- **Painting or drawing**—I can paint or draw myself or a symbol of myself with strength, impermeable to negativity or neediness of others. Circles, houses, rooms, or animals are examples of representations of myself.
- **Tidying up the house**—Sweeping floors and wiping down walls and edges of rooms can become a ritual for a vital sense of clear, solid boundaries.

OPEN SPACE

Look into your mind, your heart, your body. Write. Scribble. Color. Draw.

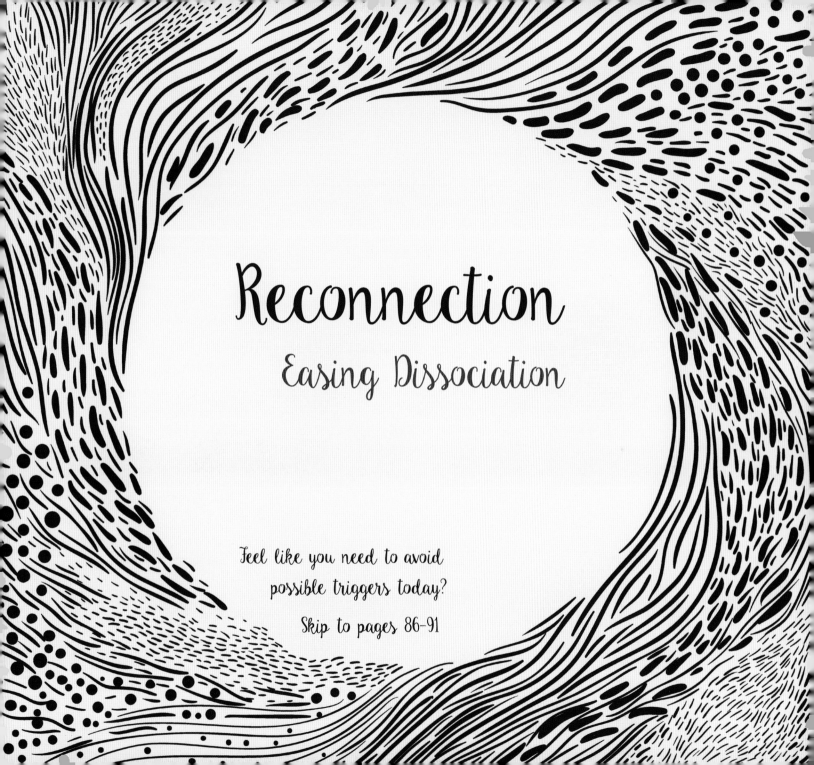

Reconnection

Easing Dissociation

Feel like you need to avoid
possible triggers today?

Skip to pages 86-91

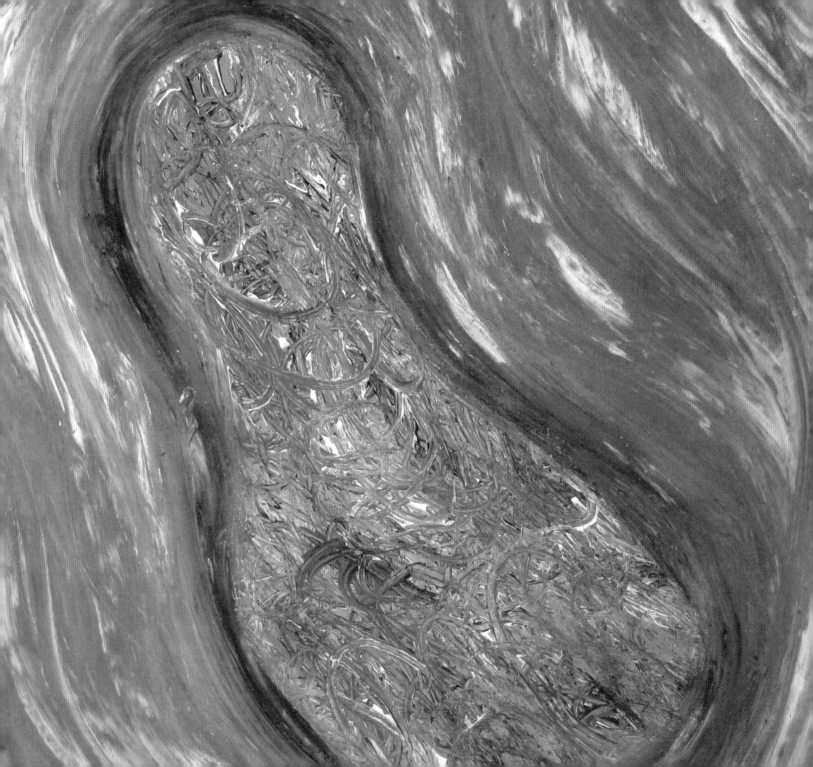

Cradling Insanity

I questioned my sanity several times during intense healing years. Repressed memories felt like insanity. My mind performed backflips, twists, and turns as I uncovered more memories. I understood why they were repressed.

The experiences were insane. *I'm not insane.*

I painted *Cradling Insanity* as I dealt with the roughest period of my healing, when the clear mental memories started to emerge. I recall lying next to my son early one morning, unable to leave his bed because he kept awakening when I did. My anxiety level was very high. I felt my head start to spin. My usual self-calming techniques like deep breathing and gently rocking back and forth weren't working. The spinning intensified. I felt as though my consciousness was going to spiral up and out of me. I reached down and firmly rubbed the soles of my feet, praying for help to keep myself grounded. Trying to keep my awareness within myself and within my present setting, I held a steadying focus on a sliver of light coming through at the edge of the curtains.

There are levels of dissociating during and after trauma. Often, I was at the level of simply not being aware of what my body was feeling. But this day, I was at risk for more serious dissociation, at the edge of blacking out from panic. I managed to make it through.

I called my therapist that day and asked her for medication. I took anti-anxiety medication for a couple months to help lessen the panic. I'd avoided medication until then; now I am so grateful I had that option to help me.

Cradling Insanity shows how much I needed to nurture this frightened young part of me. I painted the feelings of insanity as an infant, needing swaddling and rocking and loving attention.

My pelvis feels inflamed, wobbly, twisted. It's heavy like an overloaded water balloon. When I breathe and pay attention to my pelvis, I feel sadness well up, as though there's an artesian well bursting up from my lower abdomen to fill my heart with sad, sad waters. My hands feel prickly as all these waters overflow from my heart. They gush out in shaky waves down my arms and hands.

I decide to blend together some castor oil and homeopathic muscle gel. Gently, I rub this over my lower back, hips, and the front of my pelvis. I place ice packs on my pelvis and rest on the couch. The fiery feelings abate. The energy behind them cools but shifts upward through my body. I start to feel dissociated, fuzzy. I notice that my awareness of my head and eyes becomes distorted. I feel cross-eyed, with my left eye somehow out in front and higher than my right eye. I breathe. Anger prickles through the front of my head. Nausea in my stomach. Some muscles twitch in my legs. Words ride the anger in my mind. "I hate him!" "He's horrible!" "Don't listen to him!" I reach for my journal and scrawl these phrases in big, messy letters. I press hard into the paper with the pen. The rage lets go of me. I sigh and am relieved to notice the nausea is gone too.

Recognizing Dissociation

Dissociation is another common psychological term that at first seemed just that—a term, without clear real-life meanings. Dissociation covers a broad range of experiencing disconnection from oneself and the world. There are many articles and books written about the continuum of dissociation and what can be considered normal or what can be part of a disorder. In my case, dissociation seems best classified as a symptom of PTSD. Just as with warning triggers, dissociation patterns developed to protect me during abuse. My mind learned to loosen and distort awareness of my body and experience. I didn't have to feel all the horror.

My understanding of dissociation grew as I healed from trauma and became more and more connected to the present moment, my thoughts, my emotions, and my body sensations. There was a stark difference, especially in my experience of my emotions. I hadn't actually *felt* feelings as a child and young adult. Emotions had been an urge to cry or yell or run away, without any awareness that emotions also could have connections to sensations in my body.

Healing trauma wounds expanded my self-awareness. My thoughts became more clear to me. I could feel the precursors of emotions. I gradually became more adept at labeling these sensations. It was a new world of being human. Dissociation pulled me out of the present moment, back into patterns from the past, back toward emotional and physical numbness, and away from my inner capabilities of connecting with and shifting emotions.

Dissociation was terrifying for me as child. I harbored fear that it proved I was crazy. At its worst, my sense of hearing would distort, and time would stop. I would disappear and reappear to myself without a clear sense of what had happened while I was "gone." It's been so healing to understand more about dissociation as an adult, to affirm for those scared parts of myself that dissociation served as a protection for me during overwhelming abuse. My brain got those dissociative patterns so well trained that they replayed at later times, sometimes randomly and sometimes during stress or triggers.

Beyond abuse triggers, I found that using technology can chip away at a strong awareness of my body. My mind floats into an e-sphere. For some people, this escape into technology might stay on a healthy spectrum that they are able to shift out of with flexibility. For me, though, strong abuse-related dissociation patterns tend to recur when I overuse computers and other technology. It can be hard to reconnect with my body as my mind still swirls in abstract e-mode. Setting timers to take lengthy breaks from computers helps.

My experiences of dissociation vary widely. They can be very fleeting or last for weeks. Often, nausea accompanies dissociation, as though my consciousness gets motion sickness from not being fully grounded and connected to my body. Perhaps the nausea is also my body's way of recording the disgusting events even as my mind needed to completely turn away, up, and out. Anxiety also usually vibrates within and around me when I dissociate.

I accumulated a list of descriptions during the times when I didn't feel fully "in" myself:

- Dissolved boundaries, as though I am not aware of my skin as a solid container for my body
- Decreased awareness of my lower body, not feeling alive in my legs
- Disconnection from the ground beneath my feet
- Numbness in my pelvis
- Feeling "floaty"
- Feeling like I am spinning upwards and about to black out from anxiety
- Foggy brain
- Difficulty concentrating
- Slow recall of what I've done earlier that day or week

Fire Anvil Nothing Blisters Ice Dense Shocked

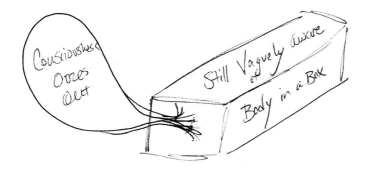

- Poor recall of my childhood
- Poor recall of my life around the time in adulthood when I was sexually violated
- Shaking out of myself in all directions
- Feeling unbalanced, often pulled to my right side
- Feeling small
- Feeling like my body's shape is distorted like Cubist paintings
- Feeling lost in time, not present
- Distortion of sounds

- Hiding deep within—a sense of being lost within myself rather than outside myself
- Unaware of my feelings or a delay in feeling emotions
- Unaware of the physical-sensation correlates to emotions
- Unaware of hunger or fullness
- Heaviness in my core keeping me from moving while I observe my immobility from above
- Feeling like my body is in a box while my head is floating and connected by a tether

CREATIVE SELF-CARE FOR DISSOCIATION

These techniques help me shift out of feeling separate from my emotions, body sensations, and the present moment.

- **Body-oriented techniques**—See Survivor's Toolbox: Easing Dissociation & Rebuilding Boundaries through the Body on page 88.
- **Drawing**—I sketch how dissociated/warped/confined/disconnected I feel. It can be difficult to describe in words, so a sketch feels more complete and validating.
- **Resting**
- **Sitting on firm surfaces**
- **Self-massage**—I use firm, deep pressure and often focus on my feet and legs.
- **Alternating foot pressure on a perpendicular surface**—I lie on a bed with a footboard and press one foot against the footboard and then the other foot, repeating for a minute. This helps me feel more settled and solid when I awaken feeling spacey and anxious. Another option is lying on the floor and pressing feet against a wall.
- **Alternate nostril breathing**—A practice from yoga traditions. I inhale through left nostril while holding the right nostril closed. Then I exhale through the right while my left nostril is closed. Next, I inhale through my right nostril while the left nostril remains closed. Finally, I exhale through the left while the right is closed. I repeat the cycle several times.
- **Downward and inward intentions**—Sometimes, exercises, dance movements, or breathing patterns work against my healing and feel destabilizing. Sexual energy is often focused upwards through the body, so traumatizing sexual energy can make upward energies feel unsafe. Dissociation is also often an up-and-out experience. By incorporating the intention and visualizations that the activity will anchor me downward and inward, I can create a more balancing activity.

- **Gardening**—Pulling weeds, sticking my hands in earth and mud, and kneeling on the ground all help pull me into a stronger sense of my body.
- **Walking in nature**
- **Breath of fire**—A yogic breathing technique in which the abdomen, especially near the diaphragm, is rapidly pulled inward toward the spine while exhaling quickly through the nose. The inhalations naturally follow the exhalations. Rapid repetition for a minute helps build some fiery energy, as courageous anger helps me feel like I can protect myself without losing touch through dissociation. To keep from feeling ungrounded, I envision the energy flowing inward and downward.
- **Avoiding caffeine, sugar, and alcohol**
- **Eating root vegetables and meat**—I have found eating root vegetables such as potatoes, carrots, beets, turnips, or any other vegetable that matures underground can be helpful. Meat also has a grounding effect on me.

"To touch the surface is to stir the depths"
—Deane Juhan

SURVIVOR'S TOOLBOX

Easing Dissociation and Rebuilding Boundaries through the Body

Try each of these techniques when you're feeling uncomfortable symptoms. Discover if one or two work better for you than others. Practice the more effective techniques four or five times a day, even at times when you feel good. Do this for three weeks, and see if you feel a difference in how you feel overall. I think these techniques gradually change the deep grooves in body/mind patterns from trauma.

Consistent repetition and incremental relief may help you reach a place where moderate trigger responses can be shifted to a peaceful state within only a minute or two.

Earth Hug

Take an old sheet or blanket outside to a fairly level spot. Lie down in whatever position feels most nurturing for you. If you feel self-conscious that people might think you're doing something strange, find a secluded spot or bring a book to set beside you—pretend you're napping after reading.

Breathe slowly. Let your body relax gradually. Surrender. Know that the small piece of ground beneath you is part of our planet. Visualize yourself as a being held lovingly by our vibrant and welcoming Mother Earth. Imagine all the pain and worries draining into the ground where it can be transformed into positive life energy.

Weighted Comfort

Place moderately heavy objects such as rocks, heavy pillows, or beanbags on your body. Fill large socks with cheap rice. Place smooth rocks into a pillowcase. Weighted blankets, vests, or small, rice-filled bags can be purchased as well. Vary amounts of time you use weighted comfort to find what works well. Try putting them all over your body while lying down. Some body regions may yield more benefit from the heavy sensation. They can be placed on your lap or thighs if you're seated.

Stretchy Bands

Physical therapy and Pilates routines utilize broad elastic bands to provide resistance during movements. While seated or lying down, experiment with holding the band with your hands and pressing your feet into it. Wrap the band around a heavy or anchored object (post, tree, heavy chair, banister rail), and pull on the band. Tie it in a loop around a stable object, and use your torso to pull on the band. Vary angles by twisting and crossing over the band. Tie it to the legs of a chair and stretch it back and forth with your feet and lower legs. Try out an exercise video that uses bands.

Pressing & Dragging[5]

A yoga mat is ideal for this exercise, but it can also be done on a firm floor like linoleum or hardwood. Wearing short sleeves and shorts, sit on the mat or floor. Lean forward and press your forearms into the mat. Pause and drag the arms slightly over the mat, so that the skin is shifted over the underlying muscles and bones. Take pauses and then press and pull in different directions. In the pause, it can be useful to take a deep breath and hold it for a few seconds. Do the same types of motion with your legs and even your back.

---

5   Chitra Giauque, School of Yoga Alchemy and Ayurveda, www.chitragiauque.com.

Tree Support

Be a Buddha and give sitting under a tree a try. I like to sit with my back to the tree, knees bent, and feet flat on the ground. This provides more stability and bit of pressure backwards into the trunk.

Push-Ups

Push-ups apply a lot of pressure to the hands, as well as activating deep core muscles. I find that perfect form isn't necessary to gain benefits. Knees can be on or off the floor. Standing up and pushing off of a wall, tree, or countertop also works.

OPEN SPACE

Look into your mind, your heart, your body. Write. Scribble. Color. Draw.

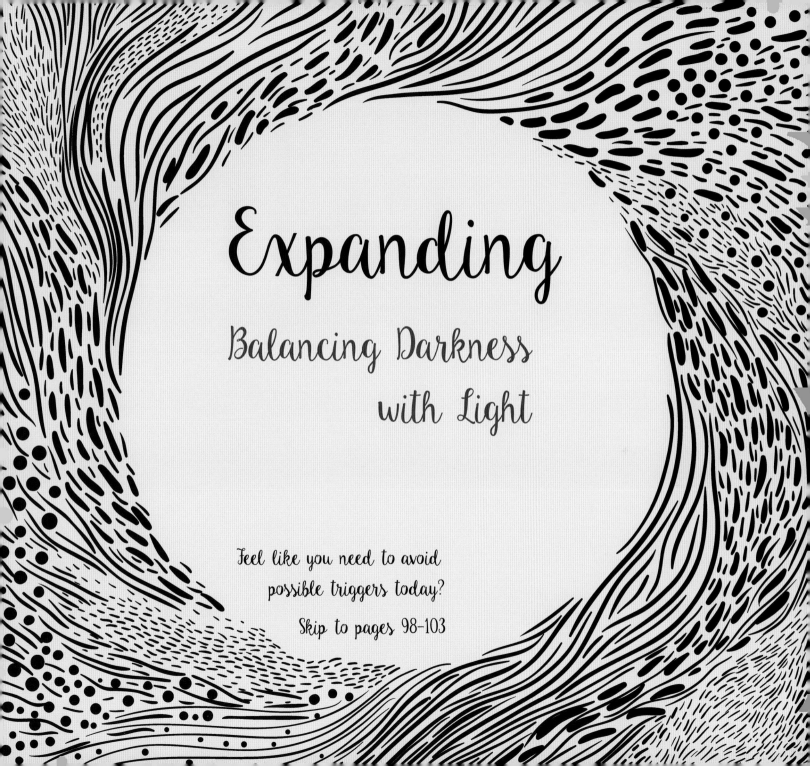

Expanding

Balancing Darkness with Light

Feel like you need to avoid
possible triggers today?

Skip to pages 98-103

Expanding

Tending my spirituality has become essential for me as I feel my way through dark days. As my emotions flow during my healing, my connection to what feels sacred grows as well. Children are sacred. Creativity is sacred. Nature is sacred. Smiles are sacred. I feel *Expanding* in my heart core, a center of pure light untouched by ugly experiences. It's what I feel is shared by all in the universe. Beauty. Light. Love. Truth.

Light Ascending

As I look at *Light Ascending*, I feel similarly to how I feel when rising out of a standing forward bend, touching my toes. There's an opening within me that expands as my body uncoils and my arms reach high overhead. That opening is the white light at the base of *Light Ascending*. The deep black seems to hold the light as it rises. Hope rises. Clarity rises. I painted *Light Ascending* early on in my healing, before I had remembered the childhood sexual abuse. The light is not only hope but also the clear light of remembering.

Honoring Light & Dark through Photography

Just as I've embraced the necessity of moving through darkness to heal, I've also learned to follow and feed sparks of hope, clarity, and light. Sometimes these sparks are dim and far, far away. I can't force myself to see beauty and peace, but I can slow down and soak in the light when it does appear around and within me. I've intentionally sprinkled soothing or uplifting photographs throughout this book to provide some respite from the heavy topic.

My camera is one of the best tools I have to amplify joy and lightness within me. Taking photographs is healing for me in ways different from painting. I paint and typically feel a cathartic release of emotions and sensations, a cleansing flow. My inner life lives outside me in the paintings. Photography reverses this direction. What is outside me enters in. I pause to take a picture and absorb the invisible message that caught my attention and reverberated internally.

Prayerful Pictures

When I see something beautiful and capture it, I'm filled with gratitude and joy. I feel an urge to reach for my camera when I feel a certain physical quiver within me, as though a greater spirit is flowing through me and turning my attention to see something sacred. And by paying homage by taking the photo, that greater spirit flows even more strongly through me. I send out gratitude in response to seeing beauty in the world. Taking pictures is a potent form of prayer for me. Many of the photos in this book feel deeply prayerful to me. Each is a little record of beauty, light, and simplicity.

Camera as Companion

I'm in the woods to find some gentleness and peace. I've been feeling very high anxiety for a couple of days. Usually, going to the woods to sit next to a stream or to lie on the earth settles my anxiety considerably. Today, there's no relief. Anxiety borders on panic. I don't know what to do. Nowhere and no one feel safe. I know I'm not going to die from the panic, yet panic can breed more panic. The rattles of anxiety keep multiplying within me. Sitting still ramps up the feelings of unease, so I pick up my camera and start photographing.

We've had a strange week of cool rain in July. Mushrooms have sprung up everywhere. Many I've never seen before. I get down on the ground and document these ephemeral, midsummer gifts. I'm amazed at how gloriously some of them pose for me. The anxiety remains, but I am alive and able to see beauty in the middle of turmoil. My camera becomes my friend, helping me view myself from a perspective of sanity despite the layers of confusing feelings. I'm able to hold on, knowing the panic won't last forever. I'm able to engage myself in photography without shutting off my awareness. This isn't always easy, and I'm not always able to go about various activities every time high anxiety overtakes me. Often I feel immobilized by fear. But staying active and creative works today.

Changing Perspectives

Photography helps me realize the ways that changing perspectives can change my inner reactions to the world.

Lie down.

Look down.

Hide behind.

Tower over.

Look up.

Ever since I was a teenager, I've loved pointing my lens at the forest ceiling. It's magical to change visual perspective in this way. The trees show their strength and delicate natures against a sky canvas. Forest sky photos bring me a sense of hope as well as a feeling of being gently sheltered.

Photos at the Edge

Sometimes I'm drawn to photograph patterns and scenes that don't spark inner gratitude for the healing beauty of the world. Instead, they resonate more darkly

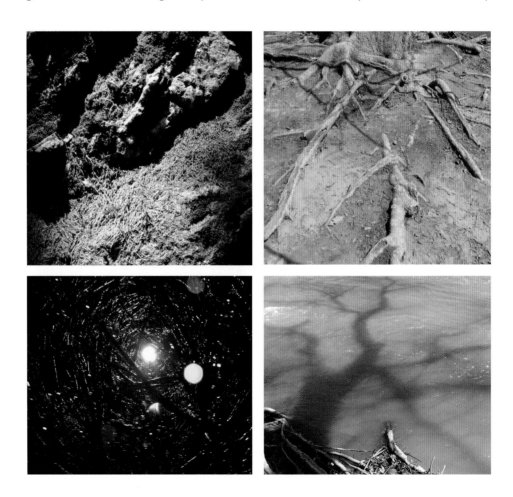

with what has been broken within me. These types of photos take me to the edge of something raw. They scratch. They unnerve.

I usually choose to look away. If I let myself gaze for a while and feel the effects, I find more details of what is untended within me. Some of it is fear. Some of it is rage. Some of it is loneliness. Some of it is wildness. Some of it is indescribable. While these photos don't soothe or restore me, they do heal by encouraging me to continue to pay attention to hidden cracks and pain. There is beauty in photos of darkness. I see it as the beauty of truth.

Reflecting Light Back into Me

It's a cool fall morning. I take my warm tea and heavy heart outside. I notice reflections of the trees in my square cup. Little jumps of recognition course through me . . . beauty . . . simplicity . . . surprise . . . time to get the camera. I carry my tea around the yard, finding new reflections to capture.

The tea grows cold, yet I am warm with a fire of creative fun. My heart grows lighter.

Witnessing What Emerges

My camera can, at times, fall into the role of friend or therapist.
I take photos of my paintings, a sketch of how I feel, a journal entry, or something else I've created. I feel more emotional completion toward what I've expressed.

It's a quiet way of saying to myself:

I see you.
I see what you've shared.
It's here.
It's okay to let it go, to let it be outside of you now.

SURVIVOR'S TOOLBOX

Nurturing Lightness

Healing from trauma involves heavy work. When I do feel more peaceful, hopeful, or joyous, I try to fully engage the feelings. Perhaps brain patterns can be retrained by immersing ourselves in happiness when possible. Simply expressing gratitude for the break in the darkness may help keep the joy around longer.

Many of these activities may seem childish because they are. Children are masters at creating lightness.

- Smile at puppies, children, adults, yourself
- Make a "happy" playlist
- Dance to upbeat music
- Soak in sunlight
- Sing
- Watch comedies and stand-up comedy
- Watch kids' movies
- Read silly children's literature
- Photograph what brings you joy or comfort
- Write wacky, rhyming poems
- Paint in vibrant colors
- Make uplifting or goofy art, and leave it in public places or out in nature
- Build a fairy house
- Watch cute animal videos online
- Eat at your favorite restaurant
- Run for fun and ask someone to chase you
- Buy flowers for yourself or someone else
- Carry vibrant essential oils with you to smell occasionally
- Make silly faces in a mirror—even better with a child there to laugh
- Draw faces on pieces of fruit and leave them in odd places
- Buy yourself toys that you remember loving as a child
- Blow bubbles and watch them float toward the sky

OPEN SPACE

Look into your mind, your heart, your body. Write. Scribble. Color. Draw.

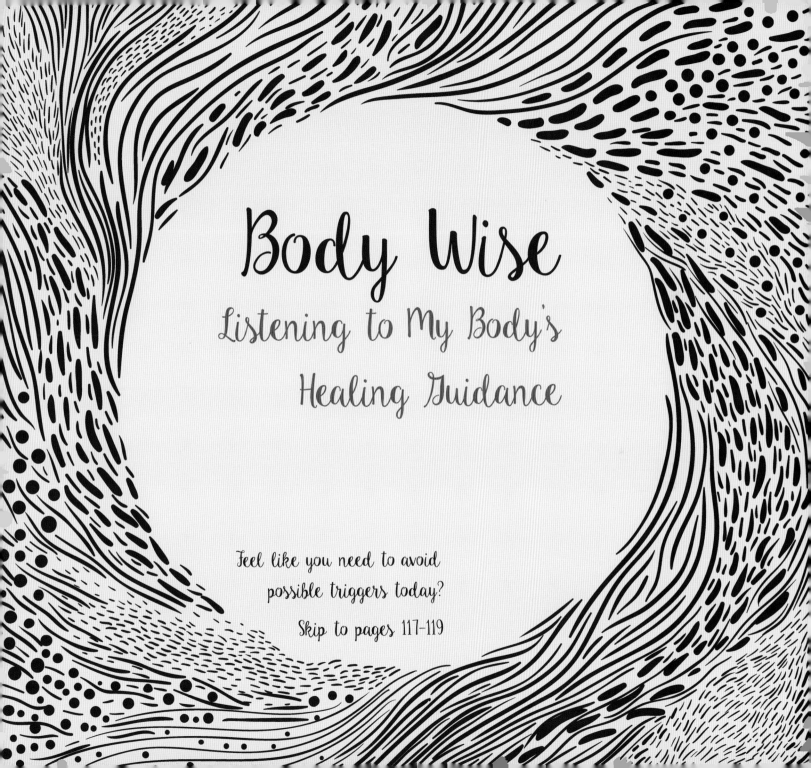

Body Wise

Listening to My Body's Healing Guidance

Feel like you need to avoid
possible triggers today?

Skip to pages 117-119

Get Out of Me

Often I paint to rid myself of an uncomfortable emotion or sensation. For a couple of years, I frequently felt nausea in my stomach area and just to the right, near my liver and gallbladder. It felt dense, a vile mass that was put there by those who sexually abused me. It felt as though tendrils radiated out from it, anchoring throughout my body. I came to imagine this as something I could cleanse and remove from my body. I gently scrubbed the skin over the gross-feeling areas with sea salt. I placed cool herbal compresses there. I got much relief from painting *Get Out of Me*.

Disgusting. Inhuman. Not me.

Fear

In alternative and complementary healthcare traditions, the kidneys and nearby adrenals are often associated with fear. At times, I could feel this on a sensation level. My body's memories of the sexual abuse sometimes began in my lower back. I'd feel the area around one or both kidneys seizing up, sending out muscle tension and a jittery energy that permeated my entire body. During one body memory, I drew *Fear*. There was sharp breast pain too.

The words I wrote on the drawing: "It feels so scary. Kidneys, especially left, squeezing out fear into my whole being. Left breast pain. This is how I feel. Jittery. Zig-zag ragged." I felt so much less pain and fear after coloring this picture.

I check my email after coming home from a lovely week of mountain camping with my son. There's a message from a person still connected to a man who abused me. I start to feel nauseated. My stomach tightens and tightens all afternoon.

By early evening, I'm throwing up. My lunch, eaten just before checking my email, was still in my stomach. Not any more though. The waves of nausea are strong, so I can't be more than ten feet from the bathroom. Thank God a neighbor is able to drop off a couple cans of Sprite. There's a part of me that feels panicked, as though the sickness will never end. I will die. Did a young Naomi feel such hopelessness? I think so. There were all those mornings of nausea for her, sometimes so strong that the motion of riding on the school bus felt overwhelming. There was the panic of not understanding the pain her body was feeling. She didn't understand what was happening to her. No one around her understood enough to support her.

And here I am now, alone and retching up vileness. I call my sister, hoping to ease the loneliness. It helps knowing she's there, an anchor for me, even though she's three thousand miles away. But when I start to tell her about the email, nausea boils over and sends me to the toilet. It continues all evening and night. I sleep upright to ease the floaty feelings. When all that emerges from me is foam and bile, I sense that this is what really wants to leave me, what has been pushing everything out ahead of it. The rational, healer part of me knows this is a cleansing purge and I will feel better after it all. But damn it, I hate it.

The next day I am so grateful to be able to sip lemon-lime soda and eat saltine crackers. A rock remains in my stomach. I feel wilted and scoured. Soon I can eat more, but I rely on foods that feel cleansing to me: potatoes, applesauce, fresh herbal teas. I feel an aversion to anything fatty.

For the next week, I feel almost hilarious rage slice through me at totally benign times. I set my water glass down on the counter, and "you piece of shit" pops into my head. I take deep breaths with my feet in a cool bath, and "I hate you all" sits on the tip of my tongue. I suppose it's related to the deep bile I literally accessed and allowed to come out of me. A couple of times, I feel the need to physically express some of the anger. I go outside and slam an old, heavy bike lock into the ground over and over and over. I am crushing those who have hurt me.

Sadness flows in fully after several days of the tense stomach and anger. This feels different. Normally I feel flattened by sadness before any anger appears. I listen to the inner four-year-old Naomi. She is sobbing. For the first time, I can imagine her turning toward me for comfort while she cries and cries. I cry and hold her, grateful she's feeling safe enough to relax into her sorrow with me. I want to get up from my bed. She doesn't want to move or be alone so we make an agreement that she can rest in a cozy backpack on my back while I work. I get my laptop and start writing this section. I am amazed at the power of visualizing my younger self, listening to her, and giving her what she says she needs to heal.

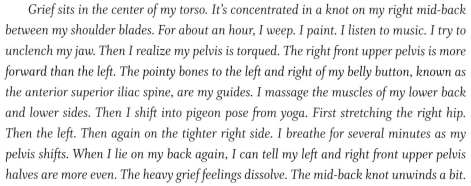

Grief sits in the center of my torso. It's concentrated in a knot on my right mid-back between my shoulder blades. For about an hour, I weep. I paint. I listen to music. I try to unclench my jaw. Then I realize my pelvis is torqued. The right front upper pelvis is more forward than the left. The pointy bones to the left and right of my belly button, known as the anterior superior iliac spine, are my guides. I massage the muscles of my lower back and lower sides. Then I shift into pigeon pose from yoga. First stretching the right hip. Then the left. Then again on the tighter right side. I breathe for several minutes as my pelvis shifts. When I lie on my back again, I can tell my left and right front upper pelvis halves are more even. The heavy grief feelings dissolve. The mid-back knot unwinds a bit.

Today, it's body-focused therapies that relieve emotional symptoms. It's as though the positions of my bones and how they tug on other areas of my body through connective tissue are the triggers or companions for feeling emotional trauma patterns.

Mapping My Body

When I follow what my body is telling me, my healing flows more easily. I learned this approach through my experience as a massage therapist and as a client of practitioners of somatic/body psychotherapy, a holistic approach in which body sensations are respected for healing guidance as much as emotions and thoughts. Trauma lands in the body, altering nervous system functioning into hypervigilance that can negatively impact other body systems. Once I learned about this perspective on trauma damage, I was able to connect the dots between so many physical sensations, ailments, emotional patterns, and mental outlooks. Books by Babette Rothschild, Bessel van der Kolk, and Peter Levine (see Resources list on page 189) helped me understand the concept of body memories, when trauma memories replay through physical sensations. It was a huge turning point in my healing journey—so much started to make sense. And once it started making sense, the trauma began to leave me.

My local rape crisis center held an art expression workshop for sexual abuse survivors. I created this body map at the workshop. It's full-size. Often for therapy sessions or for a workshop like this, my body seemed to understand I was listening for healing signals. Many signals rumbled through me that day. I used a broad brush to paint most of the background purple on my body image. I soon realized I felt physically and emotionally soothed by the gentle painting strokes. After adding in depictions of uncomfortable feelings I held within me in those moments, I switched to applying glitter in specific places needing love. I glittered a protective cleansing spiral around my body. Listening to my body, reflecting via an image, and adding in healing intentions were all very powerful for me that day.

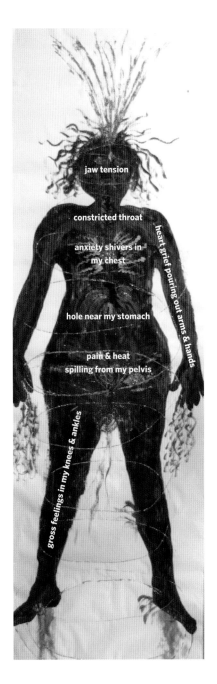

jaw tension

constricted throat

anxiety shivers in my chest

heart grief pouring out arms & hands

hole near my stomach

pain & heat spilling from my pelvis

gross feelings in my knees & ankles

Tracking my symptoms and trying different self-care techniques led me to create a comprehensive, body-based chart, seen on the following page as "Anatomy of Sexual Violation & Healing Care." Each area of my body has carried its own weight of trauma impacts, with variations on what care is needed. For more details on the self-care techniques, see the "Building a Foundation of Creative Self-Care" chapter on page 155. A blank body map on page 116 is offered as well for you to use to track your body's healing patterns and favored self-care.

Anatomy of Sexual Violation & Healing Care

Symptoms

Self-Care

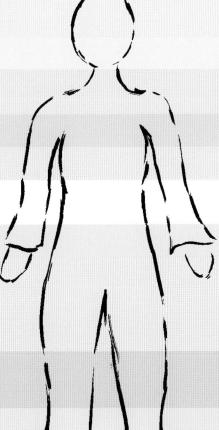

Difficulty concentrating, feeling foggy, headaches

Salt bath, lying on ground, aromatherapy, journaling, LENS, BodyTalk, brain training computer games, deep pressure, spicy or tangy foods

Tight jaw muscles, anger

Massage, hot or cool compress, yelling, hitting punching bag

Lump in throat, feeling I cannot speak of any of this, guilt, sore throat, heavy & jittery feelings, self-blame

Making sounds, punching bag, saying "No!" & "Get away from me!," painting, journaling, singing, talk therapy, or talking to a friend

Heavy, wet, jittery heart area, grief, caved-in posture, difficulty breathing deeply

Crying, lying on ground, push-ups, self-talk "I'm here with you" & "You're safe now"

Breast pain, center right back tight spot along spine

Salt scrub, cool compresses with herb plantain, yoga twists for mid-back

Nausea, anger, feeling gross, tight stomach, intense spot on right side of upper abdomen where toxic tendrils of abuse seem to reach into me

Salt scrub, holding rocks, lying on ground, herbs, cleansing foods, making sounds, breath of fire, wrapping waist snugly, deep pressure

Tight low back muscles, jittery feelings

Stretching, yoga twists, visualizations, self-talk, lying on ground, cool compresses

Hands: Clenching into fists, heat & prickling sensation in palms, tight forearms

Hands: Holding rocks, soft cloth or smooth rock to loosely hold while sleeping, clay mud, massage

Pelvis & Thighs: Cramping, diarrhea, vaginal pain, pelvic tension & pain & heaviness, torqued pelvic/hip bones, feeling sexually aroused in a disconnected way, as though it isn't my sexuality

Pelvis & Thighs: Yoga pigeon pose, yoga twists, salt bath, salt scrub, massage, heating pad, ice packs, saying "Get out of me!"

Full Body Symptoms: fatigue, heaviness, flooding emotions, superficial pinching/prickling/hot pain, feeling like I don't have a solid body

Lying on ground, salt bath, sitting at river & rocks, butterfly hug, push-ups, deep pressure, journaling, acupressure self-care routines, dancing

Knee discomfort & shakiness, a gross feeling especially on inner knees

Salt scrub, vigorous leg exercises, stomping, kicking punching bag, saying "Get off of me!"

Tight calf muscles, feeling like my legs are unable to move freely, feeling stuck in mud

Salt scrub, vigorous leg exercises, biking, stomping, kicking punching bag, saying "Get off of me!," flexing & rotating feet at ankles, massage

Inner ankle "hot spot" of discomfort, similar to inner knee gross feeling

Salt scrub, walking barefoot in mud, aromatherapy foot bath, massage

Sore feet, especially in arches

Reflexology massage/acupressure, salt scrub, walking barefoot in mud, aromatherapy foot bath

Anatomy of Sexual Violation & Healing Care

Your Symptoms   Your Self-Care

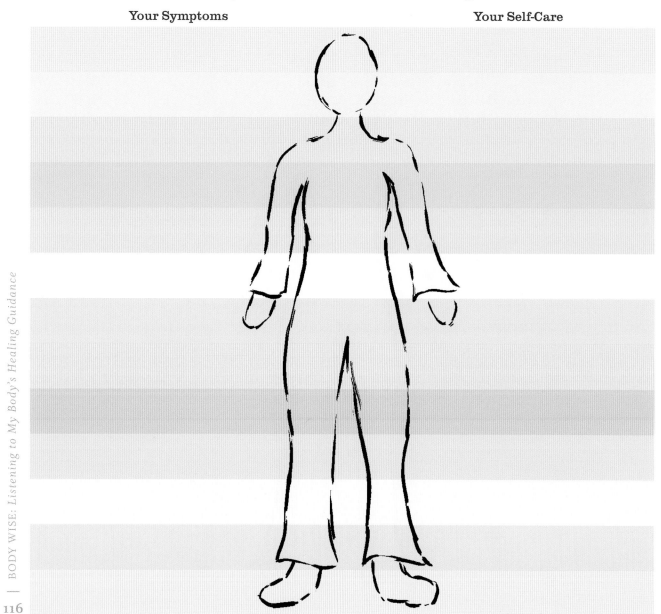

SURVIVOR'S TOOLBOX
Intuition Flowing from Inner Awareness

If you are like me, you likely received little education about intuition at home, in school, or in your culture. What does intuition even mean? Not much to someone very disconnected from her body and emotions.

When I started feeling more deeply again, both in emotions and in body sensations, the concept of intuition started making sense. I took note of when I felt internal shifts in thoughts, emotions, and sensations. Sometimes these happened when I interacted with people or when I was making a decision. I translated my inner shifts into a general yes or no and tried to follow those promptings. For a while, it felt strange and somewhat unwise based on my previous existence of trying to think my way through life and be a peacemaker at my own expense. I built up courage as my inner directions led me to greater health and peace in my life. This courage is needed because it's difficult to follow through on some intuitive signals when they aren't easily explainable to others.

So what do intuitive signals look like in me?

- Mental signals: A quick clearing of brain fog grabs my attention when it coincides with a thought. I also pay attention to ideas that repeatedly come to me. Another mental signal is when "yes" or "no" pops into my head.
- Emotional signals: When I feel anger or anxiety, I read that as a no. When I feel a grounded excitement, contentment, or calmness, I read that as a yes.
- Body sensation signals: Feeling sick or prickly or heavy usually means something isn't right for me. Goosebumps or a rain-like feeling of energy flowing downward through me usually feels like something is right to pursue. When I have options to choose from, sometimes I make symbolic markers for each option and space them out in front of me. Then I start to move toward each one, noticing how I feel inside.

Sometimes, I will feel a strong aversion to moving toward an option, as though there's a dense substance in the air blocking my path. Other times, I feel like skipping toward an option.

Here are some ways to come closer to your own intuitive guidance:

- Continually seek to deepen your inner awareness skills. Find ideas for this in the Survivor's Toolbox: Cultivating Inner Awareness on page 20.
- Create a sacred space for yourself in your home. I find that sitting in a corner of a room where I keep my inspirational books, beloved objects, and plants can help me relax and tune inward.
- Keep paper and pen by your bed to jot down any ideas that appear around waking time. Much of the content of this book flowed into being in the morning just after I awoke. New ideas seem to find me more easily then.
- Write down your dreams and ask yourself if there are any messages within them. I often have dreams that feature me paying attention to certain areas of my body. The next day, I make sure to give extra care to those areas through gentle touch, massage, stretching, etc.
- Read *Trust Your Vibes* and other books by Sonia Choquette. She teaches that all people have intuitive, or six-sensory, capabilities. We just need to learn how to listen for them and cultivate them.
- Make note of your thoughts, emotions, and body sensations when making decisions. When given choices, think about one option and notice how you feel and what thoughts come to mind. Then repeat with each option to discern which feels most right. Sometimes I trust that no options feel right at that time. Confusion can be guidance to not take action yet.

Explore your inner world and follow your intuitive signals.

OPEN SPACE

Look into your mind, your heart, your body. Write. Scribble. Color. Draw.

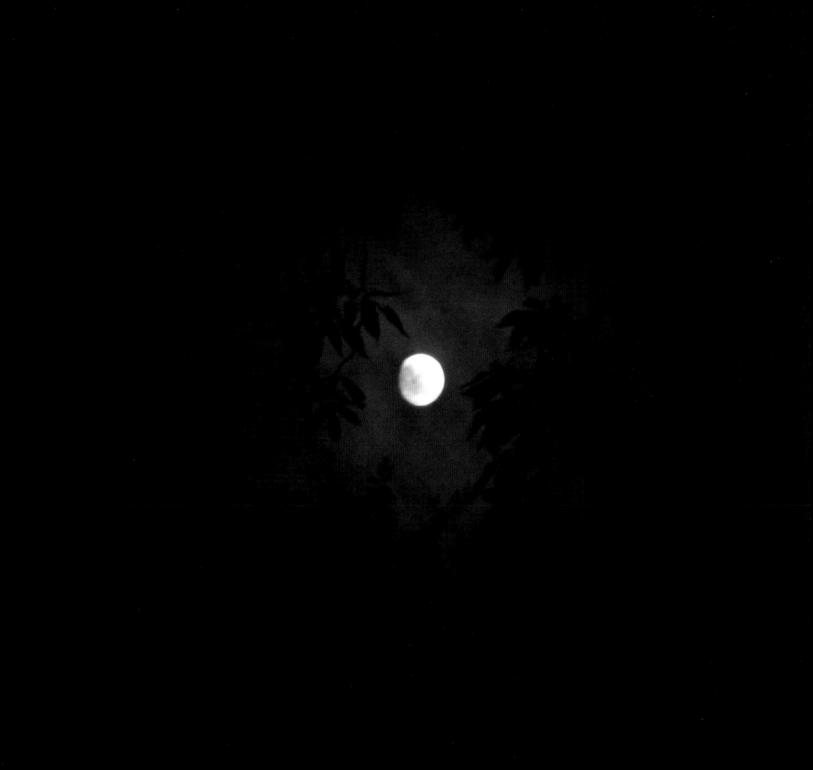

Out Rage

Honoring Truth in Anger

Feel like you need to avoid
possible triggers today?

Skip to pages 127-129

Out Rage

Out Rage probably needs little explanation. It's anger. When I painted it, I was just beginning to feel safe being angry and expressing it. *Out Rage* shows the rage created when the innocent are violated so deeply. I'm so grateful for how anger shook apart the grip of self-blame that had been suffocating me for several years. Painting helps me shift the rage outward rather than turning inward on myself. The pain isn't truly mine to hold within me. I give it back to those responsible. Or perhaps I simply release it in a cleansing way so it no longer exists anywhere or in anyone.

I feel shaky inside. Wetness rests heavily in the center of my chest. My hips and pelvis feel stiff and achy. I cry some. I feel the need to change into soft, comfortable clothes—no jeans, no snug cuffs or waistlines. I lie down in a sunny room on the floor with some cushions, as I feel like I want to avoid the bed. I rest, listening to an audiobook for company. I breathe and put one hand on my tense shoulder and one across my shaky torso. It seems a voice inside me is saying, "Please don't leave me; please don't leave me." I mentally say back to her/myself, "I'm here with you. I'm not leaving. I'm here with you. Let's rest together." I feel a bit better after about thirty minutes. I talk to my sister on the phone and feel some comfort from knowing she's reachable. Even though I feel disconnected from my stomach, I decide to cook a steak and a root veggie soup for dinner. It helps me feel grounded and less spacey. I keep the audiobook playing while I cook and clean in the kitchen.

My son has been busy at our neighborhood playground for much of the afternoon. When he returns, he does homework. I'm grateful he does not need my attention much. At bedtime, I ask him how he's been feeling. He says he's been feeling a little uneasy and sad inside. This is yet another time when I feel like he's picking up on what I'm feeling or vice versa or both. We are very connected, mom and son. I have to trust that as long as I am staying aware of my feelings and tending to them, he will not have to fully absorb and carry them too.

After he falls asleep, I go outside to the yard, lie on a blanket on the ground, and cry quietly. Some of the pressure inside my chest seems to drain into the ground. I go back inside, gather a blanket, a stuffed animal, three rocks, and a hot water bottle. I sit watching TV for about an hour, holding two rocks in my hands and one rock on my lap. I hug my stuffed animal and hot water bottle to my chest and curl my legs up into the chair.

The next morning all the chest-centered shakiness, vulnerability, and sadness has shifted toward gut-centered anger. I feel grumpy but more focused and energetic. I type out this description and then take a bike ride to work out some of the waves of rage and indignation flowing through me. This is a common healing pattern for me. Anxiety, sadness, and vulnerable feelings eventually shift into a more grounding anger.

Embracing Anger

My abuse background led to the suppression of my awareness of many emotions. I assume their intensity and continuing lack of resolution eventually led my body and mind to bury the signals of emotions. It was easier and probably wiser in my situation to block them out.

Anger, in particular, hid out deep inside for a couple of decades—likely the one emotion I knew was the riskiest to express. When I began feeling anger more fully as an adult, the experience was disorienting and scary. What were these prickly feelings spreading across my skin? These molten knots in my gut? These urges to run, hit, and kick? At the beginning of my healing journey, grief and anxiety dominated, but eventually, after working through a lot of self-doubt and self-blame, anger flared. Then I noticed that often rage felt cleansing, burning away heavy emotions and thoughts that weren't truly mine to carry.

Was I making a mistake by letting myself vent these fiery emotions? One therapist said it wasn't healthy to reinforce angry and violent behaviors. Another therapist said it was fine, that I hadn't gotten a chance to express myself as a child. Could I just skip that though? Is it somehow more spiritual or moral to let it go without getting angry? Eventually, I became convinced that my body and emotions were determining what was right for me and my healing process.

Rage was there. Rage was right. I bought a punching bag. I stomped my feet. I screamed. I imagined beating my abusers as I hit the punching bag or the futon with a thick wooden dowel I bought at the hardware store. I threw clumps of mud. I painted with reds and blacks. I cursed. I found words for what I wanted to say to the abusers:

Get the hell away from me!   *Don't touch me!*
You're sick!   *You disgust me!*
I hate you!

One winter day, I overflowed with anger. I drove to the grocery store and bought a huge plastic squeeze bottle of ketchup. I took it to the woods, found a long log on the ground, and proceeded to scream and squirt the ketchup all over the log. I screamed and screamed until all the ketchup was gone. I could then see a representation of the massacre of my soul. Blood. Old pain. Rot. Invisible turned visible and shocking. It felt soothing to then take photographs of the scene. I was witnessing and comforting the messiness and rage that I'd just released.

Intense anger coursed through me fairly frequently for about two years. Now when anger appears, it is much less potent and more easily resolved. It usually feels more related to my current life. I needed those years to purge stored feelings. I needed those years to validate my right to being enraged at all that had happened to me.

CREATIVE SELF-CARE FOR ANGER

When I need to tend anger, I rely mostly on cathartic artistic expression and body-oriented, grounding self-care.

- **Painting**—See Survivor's Toolbox for Expressive Painting with Inner Awareness on page 36.
- **Heavy lifting**
- **Biking**—I drain out anger when my feet press hard against the pedals to crest a hill.
- **Push-ups**—My hands press hard on the floor. I also push on a counter or tree for more upright variations.
- **Dancing**
- **Punching/kicking punching bag or the air**
- **Throwing**—Tossing clods of mud, heavy rice or bean-filled bags can be very cathartic.
- **Making sounds, screaming**—If I'm in a place where I can't be loud, I do silent screaming with my face in the position of yelling, mouth open and muscles clenching and then releasing.
- **Resting palms or fingers on head**—If I can sense that anger has a focal point in my head—often at the temples or mid-forehead—I place palms or fingertips on those areas. I imagine that my fingers are witnessing, validating, and comforting the angry parts of myself. I pretend I am pulling the anger out of my head and move my fingers away in a pulling motion.
- **Self-talk/affirmations**—*It's okay to be angry. I have a right to feel enraged. I'm safe when I express anger.*
- **Journaling**—I find it helpful to scrawl messy anger words in a journal. I write out what angers me, what I'm sensing in my body, and what I might say to other people if/when I feel safe enough to do so.

- **Hand mudras**—*Musti Mudra* (from the book *Mudras* by Gertrud Hirschi)—I make a moderately relaxed fist in each hand, with thumbs resting on ring fingers. Another helpful mudra involves encircling the middle finger of a hand with the fingers of the other hand. Slow deep breathing assists hand mudras in working their magic.
- **Mud**—I stick my hands or feet into mud, especially clay mud, and let it pull out uncomfortable sensations from all over my body. I use mud in nature or my yard. Clay can also be purchased from body care stores.
- **Breath of fire**—A yogic breathing technique in which the abdomen, especially near the diaphragm, is rapidly pulled inward toward the spine while exhaling quickly through the nose. The inhalations naturally follow the exhalations. Rapid repetition for a minute leaves me feeling more energized and free of whatever feelings or thoughts were plaguing me. To keep from feeling ungrounded, I envision the energy flowing inward and downward.

OPEN SPACE

Look into your mind, your heart, your body. Write. Scribble. Color. Draw.

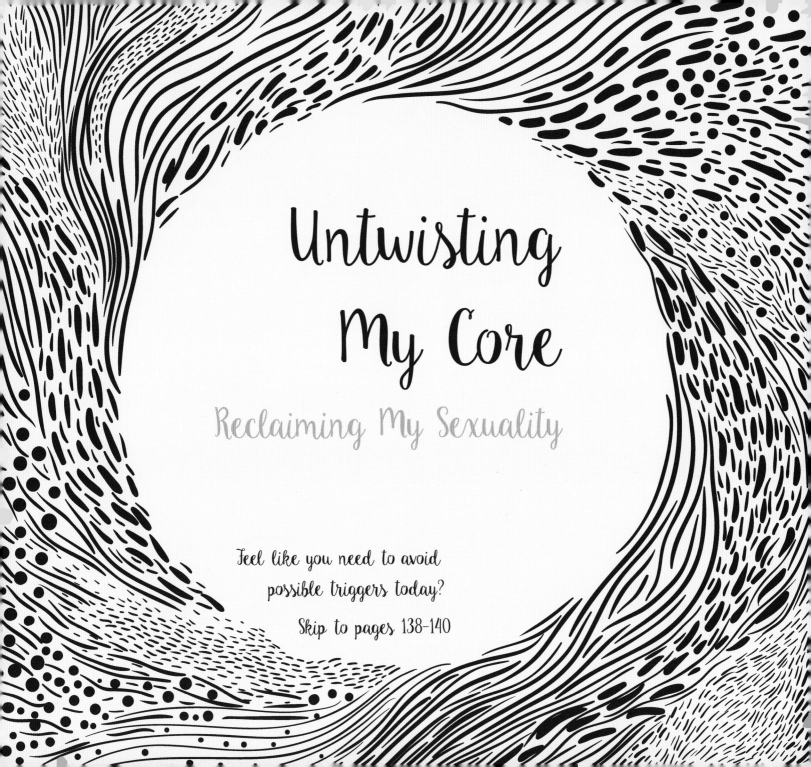

Untwisting My Core

Reclaiming My Sexuality

Feel like you need to avoid
possible triggers today?

Skip to pages 138–140

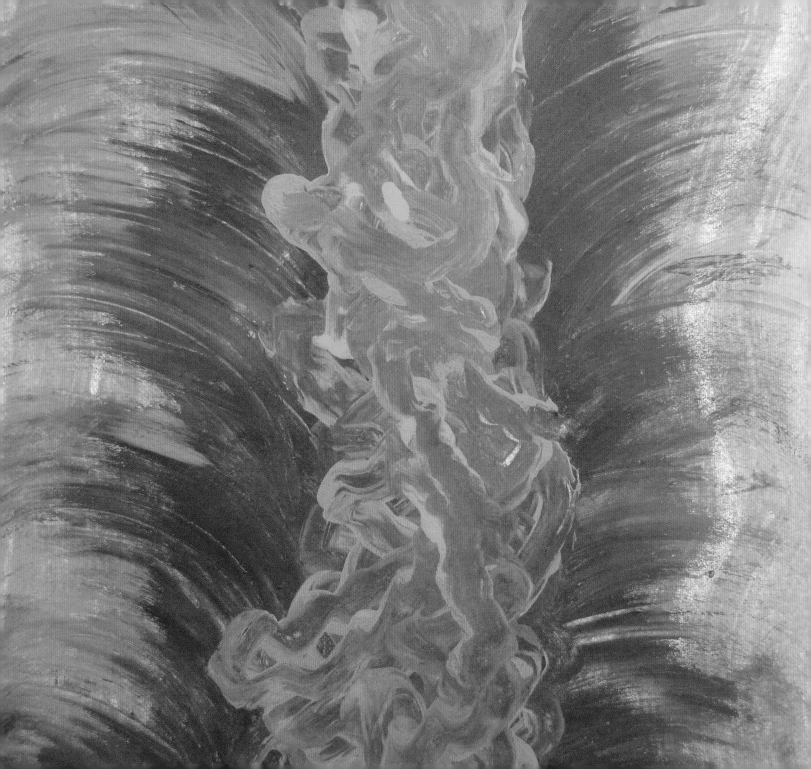

Twisted

"Paint it," said my therapist.

I'd been telling her about how twisted up I felt by being sexually manipulated by my professional mentor. It was a parallel wound, easily embedded next to the twisted knots created by childhood abuse. I went home and painted *Twisted*.

Sexuality flows most potently through our core, the center of our body and spirit. When sexuality was used as a weapon, as an adult and a child, it wounded my core. I felt lost to myself in many ways.

Who was I? Where was my core? I think about how people typically described my former mentor's behavior as "inappropriate" or "not okay." Does this painting look like the result of something *inappropriate*? Would you think to yourself, "there's a painting by a person who experienced an *inappropriate* action"?

These are weak words that don't come close to conveying the nauseating, core-twisting effects of sexualized abuses of power. *Twisted* tells of the potential damage when a trusted authority crosses boundaries with a client, student, employee, family member, or patient.

Twisted shows why ethical standards exist: to protect human hearts, bodies, and souls from harm.

Letting Light into the Depths

Letting Light into the Depths is a painting that, for a long time, elicited a painful response when I looked at it. I see a spine and pelvis in this painting, which wasn't planned but emerged as I painted.

I remember taking this painting into a therapy session soon after painting it. I cried while trying to take a deep breath into my belly as the painting seemed to encourage. My breath was meeting horrifying body sensations, left behind by childhood sexual abuse. Gradually, over years of taking healing slowly and taking breaths gingerly, I sometimes feel peace and comfort when I look at this painting.

Sexual abuse has left deep wounds in my experience of my own sexuality. In the early years of my healing, when I'd feel aroused, it felt like some outside force was feeling me up. It was charging up my body without my consent or involvement. I was faced with the conundrum of ignoring the feelings, trying to will myself to be asexual, or masturbating, which risked triggering more trauma feelings or memories.

Masturbating created high anxiety yet also felt necessary to have a sexual release. I often ended up weeping after an orgasm and wanting a cleansing bath. I needed ice packs on my pelvis to relieve congested, hot pain. At times, there seemed to be the sad, confused, hurting voice of the violated child within me saying, "Why did you do that to me?"

Definitely not the "joy" of sex.

Over time, I discovered that a three-part visualization helps avoid some of the trauma symptoms. First, I soothe the violated parts within me. I speak to my child self, as well as my young-adult self. I ask them if they'd like to spend some time in a lovely place, like the woods or playing with pets, while I'm busy doing some adult things. I listen meditatively. If they seem to say no (via a clear thought or an adverse physical sensation like nausea), then I don't masturbate, honoring their/my inner wisdom and need for a sense of safety. Usually, they seem to say yes. I imagine getting them situated and happy with an activity, companions, babysitters, or even angels. Then I return my attention to my present-day self.

In the second part of my visualization, I disconnect any mental or emotional ties to the people who have abused me. I also disconnect from anyone I sense may have sexualized intentions toward me. It usually feels right to call up some anger to set boundaries and say, "Get away from me!" I imagine them turning away and disappearing quickly far, far into the distance.

Third, I discern if I need to avoid some triggers associated with the setting. Often, it works better for me to be in a room other than a bedroom, which is associated with my abuse more than other rooms. Some days, it feels best to make a pallet on the floor and avoid beds or couches. The firmness of the floor may also aid in sensing my body and avoiding dissociation. I rarely lie on my back, as that position can still bother me. After completing a clearing visualization that shields my body and entire home, I can open the windows, spray aromatherapy, burn white sage, sing, dance, drum, ring a Tibetan singing bowl, shake rattles, or play invigorating music. I imagine brilliant lights filling my refuge, a cocoon of healthy barriers illuminating the house. I set an intention that this is my time with myself—and no one else is invited. I then return my attention to the present moment and my own sexual pleasure. Calming my nervous system over time has naturally allowed being sexual with myself to feel healthier and more enjoyable. Grief, anxiety, and shame build up infrequently alongside sexual desire. Occasionally, I feel a warm energy filling me and streaming out of my heart and hands after an orgasm. I rest and soak it in, often feeling called to place my hands gently on my head, as though self-love is healing the wounded imprints in my mind.

In order to tend newly opened wounds from sexual trauma, celibacy felt like the most healing choice for me. I needed space to heal, build my independence, and create an emotionally supportive relationship with myself. I needed to prioritize being a grounded and balanced mother for my son, without the complications of new relationships. After several years of focused healing work, I was able to consider dating. The open-heart courage needed for beginning a relationship returned to me. Finding a partner who can understand and be okay with negotiating lingering triggers and trauma patterns is key.

Allowing myself to follow my creative inspirations has also helped nourish my sexuality. Creating in the moment provides a template for how to feel more at ease with sexual energy. There is mystery, trust, and a sense of being free. Life force flows, feeding my creativity and sexuality. I am grateful to have reached a point where my sexuality no longer feels like a burden to avoid but rather a joyous part of wholeness.

For More Information

While celibacy during intense periods of healing has felt important to me, here are some resources for survivors who want to be active sexually throughout their healing.

The Sexual Healing Journey: A Guide for Survivors of Sexual Abuse by Wendy Maltz

The Courage to Heal by Ellen Bass and Laura Davis

CREATIVE SELF-CARE FOR SEXUALITY

Cleansing as well as grounding self-care techniques are usually where I turn for tending my sexuality.

- **Saying no or yes in congruence with authentic promptings**—This is a verbal way of creating boundaries and honoring when and if sexual activity feels welcome. *I have the right to decide what works for me at every moment.*
- **Downward and inward intentions**—Sexual energy is often focused upwards through the body, so traumatizing sexual energy can make upward energies feel unsafe. Dissociation is also often an up-and-out experience. By incorporating the intention and visualizations that I remain anchored downward and inward, I may be able to avoid scattered, floaty, or anxious feelings.
- **Resting palms on my body**—If I start to feel unease, sadness, anxiety, anger, etc. along with sexual arousal, I pause and try to discern where in my body these feelings are most concentrated. Then I rest a comforting hand on that spot to witness and validate the distressed parts. I don't ignore these feelings. That may lead to increased distress. I can also move my fingers in a pulling motion and imagine I'm pulling uncomfortable feelings out of my body. This may soothe me enough to continue with my desires. Other times, I need to pause and turn to other self-care.
- **Breath of fire**—A yogic breathing technique in which the abdomen, especially near the diaphragm, is rapidly pulled inward toward the spine while exhaling quickly through the nose. The inhalations naturally follow the exhalations. Rapid repetition for a minute leaves me feeling more energized and free from feeling invaded. To keep from feeling ungrounded, I envision the energy flowing inward and downward. I use this technique before sexual activity to feel free of mental ties to abuse.

- **Salt scrub**—This is helpful before or after sexual activity when any parts of my body feel heavy or tainted. In the shower, I mix a little water with coarse or fine sea salt and gently scrub any areas that feel uncomfortable, often my stomach, pelvis, or upper chest. I may add olive oil or herbs from my garden to the salt mixture. I scrub briefly, for less than a minute, to avoid damaging my skin. Then I rinse it off.
- **Salt bath**—I add a half to one cup of sea salt (coarse or fine) to the bath for a five- to twenty-minute soak. Very cleansing and refreshing before or after sexual activity.
- **Aromatherapy**—I choose essential oils based on what I'm drawn to and how I feel after smelling the oil. Cleansing eucalyptus, grounding frankincense, and uplifting citruses work well for my sexuality self-care. I add them to salt baths or put a drop in my hair.
- **Hot/cool compresses**—When sexual activity brings up discomfort, hot or cold compresses can soothe headaches, pelvis pain, chest restriction, and muscle tension.

OPEN SPACE

Look into your mind, your heart, your body. Write. Scribble. Color. Draw.

Returning

Relying on the Healing Powers of Nature

Feel like you need to avoid
possible triggers today?

Skip to pages 149-153

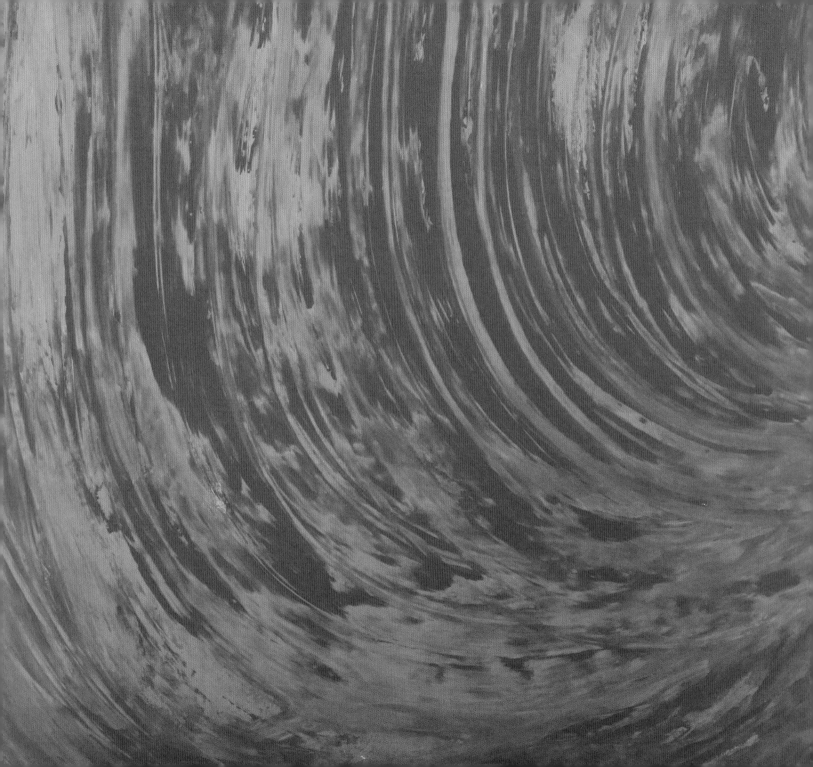

Forest Path

I feel a call to enter this painting—a forest offering comfort and direction. Down the forest path of my life, more awaits. I love the flowing, soothing colors so much that I hung it in my living room. I recall feeling a strong sense of "stop" when it was complete. "Stop, don't touch it anymore. Feel the waves of blue and green."

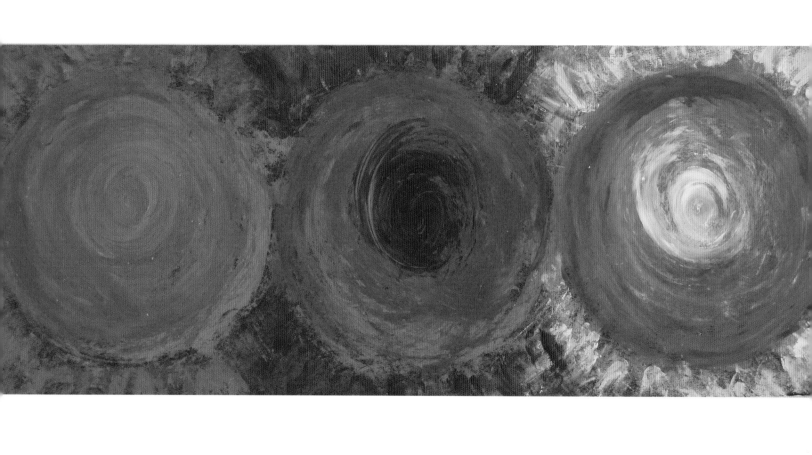

Three Earths

I rely on nature for comfort and to enliven me. I'm most at home sitting on a boulder next to a tree-lined river. I feel grief about the abuse our modern lifestyles inflict on our planet. This painting began as three blue-green circles. Then I saw they were Earths. The first became the unspoiled green planet. The second became the current Earth, with humans dramatically altering the climate and landscapes. Humans are in conflict. Species are disappearing. The third Earth is a prayer for people to shift into harmony with the planet and with each other. The three Earths are me as well: an unspoiled innocent me, a violated me needing deep healing, and the future peaceful me. Microcosm meeting macrocosm. Power abused on a personal and planetary scale. People taking what they want and not caring enough about the impacts.

It's late afternoon on a day that has felt too busy. Too many transitions in and out of the car. Too many people wanting my attention. Every few minutes, a pinching, superficial pain flickers through my whole body. I turn off the radio. I need quiet and stillness to try to stave off stronger, sustained pain. I realize I have two hours of solo time. I put on my swim clothes and drive thirty minutes to my beloved river. The vibrations and noise of the car irritate my nervous system so that the pain intensifies, but it's a trade-off I take, knowing how soothing the river can be. I arrive and just being in the forest pulls heaviness from me. I hike a few minutes to my favorite spot. A pebbly river bank. A waist-deep pool. Rocks creating a not-too-noisy rapids and mini-waterfall.

Tears flow as I gradually step into deeper and deeper water. I hadn't realized the heaviness was sadness until the river encouraged me to feel more deeply. Painful prickles and pinches lose intensity and disappear as the cool water flows past my skin. I sit on a rock and feel layers and layers of grief leave my body. It's been a summer of needing this gentle river friend to help me reset out of chronic pain and fatigue patterns. The river and rocks and green shade teach my nervous system how to find calmness again.

Nature as Healing Ally

My childhood in the woods of the Ozark Mountains connected me deeply with the earth. It was there that I first started learning about the confluence of nature, creativity, and healing. I rested in the forest. I climbed trees. I built forts and pine needle homes. As I grew, the mountains shaped my inner landscape and became a spiritual anchor. I was nourished by the overlapping blue-gray lines of distant ridges across valleys. The dirt roads, cool, north-facing slopes, hidden hollows, and my finely honed sense of direction are symbols I've returned to throughout life in thoughts and dreams. When faced with deep trauma wounds, it was clear that to heal my core, I needed to return to the support of mountains and forests and rivers. It is as though the ridges and recesses of my heart and body aligned perfectly with the folds of the mountain landscape. I could rest there more deeply. My wish is that everyone gets to experience a profound, supportive connection with our planet.

Sexual violence is sensory violence, so in order to overcome trauma, healing sensory experiences are needed. Nature offers some of the most healing sensory inputs. Humans evolved with natural elements. Our sensory capacities via skin and nervous system developed as we interacted with dirt, wind, water, fire, stone, wood, and leaves—not with steel, polyester, drywall, and plastic. When I'm in a park or forest or ocean, I sense a breathing space for my nervous system. Letting myself *be* in nature helps to reorganize and refuel a traumatized and nature-starved nervous system, allowing it to heal among sensory inputs that resonate more agreeably with my human animal nerves.

Ayurvedic medicine, traditional Chinese medicine, and Native American traditions all place high value in natural elements such as fire, earth, water, air/wind, wood, metal, and ether/space. These elements are not separate from us. Qualities of the elements reveal themselves in our temperaments and our emotional, physical, and spiritual health. By thinking about what element I might be overexpressing or underexpressing, I can seek more balance. When my nerves feel fiery, cool water and calm environments help. When I'm lethargic, fiery and airy activities like dancing may help. When I feel spacey, grounding techniques are called for to boost the earth element. It is an ever-changing balance, just as in nature.

Landscapes, plants, and wildlife support me physically and spiritually. I like to think that nature is rooting for humans to heal so that we stop creating so much pain and destruction on the planet.

CREATIVE SELF-CARE FOR CONNECTING WITH NATURE

Many of the techniques in the "Building a Foundation of Creative Self-Care" chapter on page 155 are nature-based. These are some of my favorite ways to soak in nature's healing gifts.

- **Being outside**—I find a tree, a rock, a patch of grass, a park, or a wilderness. I breathe, walk, run, and rest.
- **Lying on the ground**—I usually have my water resistant picnic blanket handy at home and in the car for this.
- **Holding rocks or placing them under my feet**—Rocks can even be purchased at arts & crafts stores in the floral section.
- **Sitting with my back supported by a tree or boulder**
- **Building a fire**—Tending a fire can empower and comfort me. Sometimes I build one with the intention of letting it help me tap into some needed fiery emotions. I also benefit from writing down emotions or situations and then burning the paper to help me clear the problems.
- **Seeking out water**—Even when it's too cold to wade or swim, just being around natural water features can feel cleansing.
- **Walking barefoot outside**—I seek out soft grass or moss or mud.
- **Bringing nature inside**—I welcome plants, rocks, sticks, and leaves into my home. I make art with them, use them in a table centerpiece, or set them on a shelf.
- **Visiting natural home habitat**—For me, green mountains are home. I go to mountains as often as possible to refuel my spirit. For others, natural home may be wide-open plains or the desert or the seashore. When it's not possible to physically be there, photos and videos are good ways to tap into those same feelings of support.

- **Gardening**—Tending plants indoors or outdoors can feel nourishing. It's a ritual that gives gratitude to the natural world. It also models how to lovingly care for myself as a living being on the planet, too.
- **Walking in nature**
- **Forest bathing**—The Japanese have a term, *shinrin-yoku,* that translates as "forest bathing." The concept resonates deeply with me, as I find much relief, comfort, and invigoration when I spend time in the woods.
- ***ReTurning* album**—This meditative music by Jennifer Berezan was recorded in an ancient underground temple in Malta. The lyrics encourage a soulful reconnection to the earth.

OPEN SPACE

Look into your mind, your heart, your body. Write. Scribble. Color. Draw.

Building a Foundation of Creative Self-Care

I have learned to prioritize taking care of myself. Providing time and space to tend to my needs is vital. Indeed, it's the only way to work toward a healthier and more resilient version of myself. I feel twinges of guilt and self-judgment about not doing as much as I "should" in my home and work lives sometimes, but now I view those judgments as damaging. I try my best to change those attitudes when they pop up in my mind. Women have often been socialized and have absorbed society's messages that we're here solely to serve others' needs and wants. I cannot give to others when my own well is poisoned or dry. In an interview with a rape survivor, television journalist Melissa Harris-Perry said to her, "It's okay to take the time you need to heal."[6]

Amen.

Resting: The Core of Self-Care

Looking at my long lists of self-care techniques, it may appear that I've been very, very busy. In reality, resting is the most important tool in my healing toolbox. I believe my body knows the path toward health and can guide me there more easily when I provide myself ample time to rest. Regular pauses—even for only two minutes—throughout the day help me feel more energetic and balanced. I try to create space for slower transitions between activities.

---

6   Jamil Smith, "Rapist's light sentence prompts survivor to go public," *MSNBC*, November 24, 2013, http://www.msnbc
      .com/melissa-harris-perry/no-prison-time-rape-survivor-speaks-out.

Resting is an integral step in much of my self-care, whether it happens before, during, or after techniques. It takes courage to rest and remain aware of what feelings, sensations, and thoughts are percolating. Sometimes, these pauses take me closer to what is next up in my healing journey, and that can feel scary. Resting also serves as time and space to become a comforting presence for myself. I speak to myself and touch my body as though I'm a trusted, gentle guide who knows what is needed, what to say, and what not to say. My body needs quiet time to adjust to the changes brought by tending trauma wounds. Over time, my need for extra rest and other self-care has diminished as my wounds healed.

An Intuitive Approach

In my healing, creativity has flowed as my emotions have flowed. I've learned to trust my creative impulses. They lead me to new ways of caring for myself. Gathering healing ideas from others helps, yet I've learned to take time to ask myself what I need. I call the answers "my intuition," a place within where I can turn for guidance. The more I follow the innate creative answers (no matter how minor, silly, strange, or embarrassing they seem), the faster I heal and the more easily my intuitive guidance comes.

Abuse can separate a person from her inner "yes" or "no." When I was forced to do things against my will, I lost touch with a capacity to know on a gut level what was right and wrong for me. After I practiced asking myself for direction and paying attention to all the cues, I gradually rebuilt my inner compass.

To do this, I typically choose to sit in stillness. I breathe. I ask, in my head or out loud, "What would feel helpful now?" Sometimes, I claim my direction: "I am connecting with my inner guidance to help me shift these (naming specific feelings, thoughts, pains, sensations, etc)." Then I meditate and listen. I close my eyes and imagine looking down into my inner body. I may feel as though a gentle rain pours through me. Thoughts, feelings, sensations, or urges to move a certain way or to do something may then arise from within. I trust those promptings as my answers. I journal if a lot of thoughts or emotions arrive. If nothing appears, then I simply monitor my thoughts and feelings for the next several hours.

The intuitive answer may suggest a sensory experience that is the opposite of how I feel inside, such as a cool compress on my inflamed pelvis or bicycling when I feel unbalanced or spacey. Other times, rather than directly trying to shift how I feel, I need to give patient attention, space, and expression to my feelings, which very often can shift the feelings too.

Tuning into my intuition works not only during meditative stillness but also during other activities that bring me closer to a more vibrant version of myself: biking, taking a shower, dancing, napping, etc. By incorporating a few minutes of asking and then inward noticing before, during, and/or after these activities, I've honed in on my more effective ways of tapping into my intuition.

Respect for Cultural Traditions

Some of these self-care techniques, such as chanting, fire ceremonies, and smudging, come from the traditions and practices of religions and native peoples. I'm not a member of these traditions. My northern-European heritage has lost much of its spiritual and healing connections to natural elements and creative expression. So I educate myself before practicing techniques from other cultural traditions. I strive to respect their origins and protocols as I apply them to my own healing process. While my personal practice may not be as authentic as if I'd been raised and trained in these traditions, there is a universal connection within practices that align with natural elements. The earth's healing gifts are meant for all, and I'm grateful we now live in a world where different peoples with different traditions can share powerful practices with each other.

Self-Care Techniques

As I accumulated a long list of what helps me feel more solid, secure, and calm, I discovered similarities and patterns. I categorize my self-care techniques into four groups:

- Deep Pressure to Ease Dissociation
- Grounding
- Rebalancing Brain & Body
- Cleansing

Next to each category, there is space for you to write notes from trying techniques that appeal to you.

Deep Pressure to Ease Dissociation

Before being sexually violated as an adult, I'd never realized how dramatically a person could shift into a different experience of herself and the space around her. I felt shattered, buzzy, ripped open, burning, oozing, fluid, and spacey—a constant disorientation for over a year. My solid body had dissolved under the touch of an abusive person.

A turning point came when I read *My Stroke of Insight: A Brain Scientist's Personal Journey* by Jill Bolte Taylor. My sense that I didn't have a solid body, my ultrasensitivity to other people's feelings and stress, my pain and fatigue, and my experience that sensory stimuli felt painfully "amped up" were similar to the experience Taylor describes. Somehow, although it was through body-focused, emotional trauma and not a stroke, the somatosensory cortex and parietal regions of my brain were not functioning as before. I then began to shift out of the perspective that I was to blame and stuck with feeling like that forever. I started to understand that harm had come to my brain functioning. Dr. Taylor had healed herself.

So could I.

I consulted with a neurologist and received an MRI to ensure no structural issues were creating my symptoms. In addition to all the body pain and fatigue, I'd had headaches, sensations of pressure, and even buzzing in those regions of my head. The MRI came back normal.

I researched brain anatomy and functioning. In chapter two of *The Brain That Changes Itself* by Norman Doidge, the author tells the story of Barbara Arrowsmith Young, a woman who developed brain training exercises to heal her own serious learning disabilities. I found hope in Young's description of how, as she strengthened certain regions of the brain, she felt more emotional resiliency as well. I just needed to find what activities could strengthen my brain's weakened areas. Then maybe the emotional floods would subside too. While Jill Bolte Taylor received massage therapy to redevelop her sense of her body's boundaries, touch as a trauma trigger made that healing route unavailable to me. I realized that some of my effective self-care was probably already healing those brain areas. My relief, as I would lay on the ground and place rocks on my body, might have been coming from providing a sensory experience of solidity. I was potentially reactivating the orientation association cortex, a region in the brain's parietal lobe that gives us our experience of physical boundaries and where we are in space.

A few studies of sexual abuse survivors show asymmetry in the size and activity of the parietal regions of the brain.[7] Dissociation processes for all sorts of emotional traumas may involve atypical

7   Landré L, et al. 2012. "Working memory processing of traumatic material in women with post-traumatic stress disorder." J Psychiatry Neurosci Feb;37(2):87-94; Irle E, et al. 2005. "Reduced size and abnormal asymmetry of parietal cortex in women with borderline personality disorder." Biol Psychiatry Jan 15;57(2):173-82; Irle E, et al. 2007. "Size abnormalities of the superior parietal cortices are related to dissociation in borderline personality disorder." Psychiatry Res Nov 15;156(2):139-49; Bremner JD, et al. 2004. "Neural correlates of the classic color and emotional stroop in women with abuse-related posttraumatic stress disorder." Biol Psychiatry Mar 15;55(6):612-20.

activity and/or reduced size of the parietal regions.[8] Interestingly, the reduction of parietal region activity was also observed in meditating monks and nuns who report feeling at one with God.[9] Perhaps this explains my—and perhaps Jill Bolte Taylor's—deeper felt experience of spirituality that has been an asset during trauma healing. While it can feel supportive to actively choose to meditate and merge with the universe and then return to non-meditative state of being, being pushed out of one's body by a sexual violation is anything but supportive. Finding one's way back into a solid and secure experience of being in one's body can be a long process. Living in the world and interacting comfortably with people demands being grounded and solid.

Occupational therapists use deep pressure therapies such as weighted blankets and vests to help calm children with autism, sensory processing disorder, and other developmental disabilities.[10] Companies that sell weighted blankets list anecdotal evidence from customers who find relief from PTSD.[11] Touch research shows a decrease in the stress hormone cortisol and an increase in calming neurotransmitters during massage therapy.[12] While some of this effect may be from the caring contact of another person, some of it may come from the moderate pressure on the skin and

8   García-Campayo J, et al. 2009. "Brain dysfunction behind functional symptoms: neuroimaging and somatoform, conversive, and dissociative disorders." Curr Opin Psychiatry Mar;22(2):224-31; Lanius RA, et al. 2005. "Functional connectivity of dissociative responses in posttraumatic stress disorder: a functional magnetic resonance imaging investigation." Biol Psychiatry Apr 15;57(8):873-84.

9   Newberg A., E. D'Aquili, V. Rause. 2001. Why God Won't Go Away. New York: Ballantine, pp. 3-8.

10 "IAN Research Findings: Occupational Therapy," Autism Speaks, February 13, 2008, http://www.autismspeaks.org/news/news-item/ian-research-findings-occupational-therapy.

11 "Springing Forward … Help For PTSD, Anxiety and Depression," Mosaic Weighted Blankets, March 9, 2014, http://blog.mosaicweightedblankets.com/springing-forward-help-for-ptsd-anxiety-and-depression/.

12 Field T, et al. 2005. "Cortisol decreases and serotonin and dopamine increase following massage therapy." Int J Neurosci Oct;115(10):1397-413.

underlying tissues. Light pressure massage does not create the same benefits as massage with more pressure.[13]

When I feel more solid and aware of my body, my hypersensitivity to sensory stimuli such as sound and people's energies decreases to comfortable levels. I also feel less full body pain and fatigue after giving a boost to my brain's awareness of my boundaries. Here are my ways of feeding the parietal regions of my brain:

- **Lying on the ground**—I usually have my water resistant picnic blanket handy at home and in the car for this.
- **Holding rocks or placing them under my feet**—Hands and feet have lots of nerve endings, so perhaps the signal of "solidity!" gets sent more strongly to the brain from these areas of skin. Perhaps this is my reinterpretation of the reason why some people like the soothing ritual of rubbing a "worry stone" into their palm.
- **Rocks on my body**—I especially like to lie on the ground on my stomach and place rocks on my back.
- **Rice/bean bags on my body**—These are easily made into a variety of sizes using pillowcases. At different times, different sizes/weights feel more effective. Great for kids too, as a relaxing time to settle inward.
- **Back to a hard wall, tree, or boulder**
- **Heavy lifting**
- **Massage**—I benefit from nurturing touch from myself, a compassionate and calm friend, or a licensed massage therapist. In order to avoid triggering trauma patterns, I always honor my inner "no" or "stop" if the touch does not feel supportive.

---

13 Field T, et al. 2010. "Moderate pressure is essential for massage therapy effects." Int J Neurosci May;120(5):381-5.

- **Pressing/dragging on yoga mat**[14]—With bare forearms and lower legs, I press and drag my arms, legs, back, or belly across a yoga mat on a hard floor. Slight stickiness of a yoga mat provides a drag to the skin surface, possibly activating different deep pressure nerve receptors. The emphasis is on the pressure, with the drag being a very short distance. Without a yoga mat, floors such as linoleum can also work well. Even just three minutes of this can lessen my anxiety and spacey-ness.
- **Pilates foam roller over back, hips, legs**—I place the cylindrical roller on floor or mat and let gravity press me down into the roller as I shift and roll.
- **Yoga poses with pressure into mat**—Deep pressure from regular yoga poses may be a factor in how yoga can be so relaxing. Most helpful for me is the hip-opening pigeon pose with dragging pressure down through front lower leg and knee.
- **Biking**—Benefits are enhanced when my feet are pressing hard against pedals while going uphill.
- **Push-ups**—Hands press hard on the floor. I also push on a counter or tree for more upright variations.
- **Pushing on car door and steering wheel in car**—Hands, forearms, sides of legs press on the interior of the car.
- **Painting**—Pressing hard onto paper on a table or floor can create sensory input through my hands as I paint.
- **Swimming in flowing water**—Swimming or just standing in a flowing stream or river provides gentle pressure on the skin in ways a pool or lake doesn't. Pool or lake swimming

14 Chitra Giauque, School of Yoga Alchemy and Ayurveda, www.chitragiauque.com.

sometimes feels too floaty and dissociating, while being in a river helps me feel more solid and relaxed.

- **Elastic band movements**—Stretchy elastic bands used in physical therapy can serve as a taut yet flexible object in which to press my hands, feet, or body. The less stretchy, tighter versions work better for me. Pressing into these feels womb-like.
- **Wrapping waist/pelvis/chest snugly with fabric**
- **Tucking in pillows/sheet/blanket**—I rest with less anxiety in bed when I can feel pillows and a heavy blanket lining my sides and back.
- **Pressing soles of feet onto a perpendicular surface such as a bed's footboard or a wall**
- **Punching/kicking punching bag**
- **Resting palms on parietal areas of head**—I place palms on back upper sides of my head and feel the firmness of the skull. I envision gentle comforting energy flowing from my heart to hands to brain.

Your Notes

DEEP PRESSURE TO EASE DISSOCIATION

Your Notes

Grounding

The terms "grounded" and "grounding" held only vague meanings for me until my own emotions and inner body sensations became more clear to me. Feeling grounded means I'm aware and feel connected to my lower body, in the same way that I feel aligned with my head and mind. Sometimes I feel grounded as what feels like a calming river flows downward through my body and into the earth. When I feel shaky, I equate that with being ungrounded. Spending too much time at a computer can lift my attention out of my lower body and more into my head, which results in an "out of balance" sensation. At times, being in crowds or talking with people I feel uneasy around can also bring this feeling of disconnection from the earth. Any experience that is a trauma trigger can make me feel as though I'm not grounded.

What I've discovered is that usually any uncomfortable "triggered" feelings or thoughts are accompanied by feeling ungrounded. I can choose to tend the feelings or thoughts, and that can help reground me. Alternatively, I can focus more on regrounding techniques, and that can help soothe the triggered feelings or thoughts. These are my most used grounding techniques:

- **Lying on the ground**—I rest on a blanket or directly on the ground. Surrendering, tummy-side down, into the earth is a potent self-care technique for me.
- **Sitting with my back to a tree or boulder**
- **Squeezing a yoga block between thighs**[15]—I also use a firm rolled up towel. I place the yoga block or towel between my thighs and squeeze while inhaling, holding in my breath for a few seconds, and contracting my pelvic floor muscles (Kegel exercises). Then I exhale, relax muscles, and repeat several

15 Chitra Giauque, School of Yoga Alchemy and Ayurveda, www.chitragiauque.com.

times. Lower points—on low thighs, knees, calves—also benefit from this exercise.

- **Walking barefoot inside and outside**
- **Walking on soft, cool moss or grass**
- **Hand mudras**—I adore these fascinating simple techniques from yoga traditions. One grounding mudra (or energy lock) is to place tip of ring finger in center of palm, with pinky extended, and other two fingers and thumb touching each other at tips. I breathe slowly and hold the position for a few minutes.
- **Arch support inserts**—When my feet receive even support, the rest of my body can align more easily.
- **Imagery of my roots growing downward**—I envision roots connecting deeply into the earth through meditation or drawing exercises.
- **Downward and inward intentions**—Sometimes, exercises, dance movements, or breathing patterns work against my healing and feel destabilizing. By incorporating the intention and visualizations that the activity will anchor me downward and inward, I can create a more grounding activity.
- **Gardening**
- **Walking in nature**
- **Avoiding caffeine, sugar, and alcohol**
- **Eating root vegetables and meat**—I have found eating root vegetables such as potatoes, carrots, beets, turnips, or any other vegetable that matures underground can be helpful. Meat also has a grounding effect on me.

Your Notes

Rebalancing Brain & Body

Early on in my healing, the first clue that my brain needed more balance between the left and right hemispheres was that the right side of my body had much more pronounced pain and tension patterns than the left side. For much of my healing, I didn't know that chronic pain—without an obvious physical cause—is common for trauma survivors. There are now studies that document that close to thirty percent of survivors experience chronic pain after sexual violation.[16] I wept the day I heard a discussion of this research on our local radio station. For many years, I kept my strange full-body pain patterns a secret from most people in my life. Because I hadn't heard or read of "valid" medical research into pain after sexual abuse, I assumed, almost unconsciously, that people would categorize my symptoms as created by mental problems and, therefore, not real. I feel deep gratitude to the physicians willing to open their minds to finding the very real nervous system impacts of trauma. Other studies even point to potential genetic influences into why some victims develop pain patterns while others do not.[17]

Left and right brain hemisphere communication flows through the corpus callosum, which may be reduced in size in abuse victims.[18] The hippocampus is reduced in size as well.[19] These changes

---

16 Ulirsch JC, et al. 2013. "Pain and somatic symptoms are sequelae of sexual assault: Results of a prospective longitudinal study." Eur J Pain Sep 10.

17 Bortsov AV, et al. 2013. "Polymorphisms in the glucocorticoid receptor co-chaperone FKBP5 predict persistent musculoskeletal pain after traumatic stress exposure." Pain Aug;154(8):1419-26.

18 Kitayama N, et al. 2007. "Morphologic alterations in the corpus callosum in abuse-related posttraumatic stress disorder: a preliminary study." J Nerv Ment Dis Dec;195(12):1027-9; Rüsch N, et al. 2007. "Corpus callosum abnormalities in women with borderline personality disorder and comorbid attention-deficit hyperactivity disorder." J Psychiatry Neurosci Nov;32(6):417-22.

19 Andersen SL, et al. 2008. "Preliminary evidence for sensitive periods in the effect of childhood sexual abuse on regional brain development." J Neuropsychiatry Clin Neurosci Summer;20(3):292-301.

in brain structures and functions match up with many of my symptoms.

Besides pain, other brain-related challenges I faced were difficulties with concentrating, reading, doing math calculations, and even finding words to make conversation. Fatigue put me in a mental fog. I couldn't multi-task or shift my attention easily. I often felt split: head from body, left side from right side. Physical coordination for sports or dancing was impaired, as though my legs and feet were poorly connected and weighted down.

I noticed improvements in these symptoms as I practiced self-care that moved the body in left/right connection patterns. Other improvements came with more brain-focused exercises. Here's a list of what helps me:

- **Brain training games**—I have an account on lumosity.com for computer games that work various brain functions. Games that encourage flexibility through shifting tasks repeatedly have helped the most. I find anxiety can be reduced by playing just a few minutes.

- **Butterfly hug**—By crossing arms in front of my chest, I tap first on one shoulder and then on the other. This gets the left and right brain hemispheres communicating. Uncomfortable emotions and sensations seem to drain out of me. It works on chest, hips, and legs, as well as shoulders. This is most effective when I can turn my attention softly inward. This exercise comes from Eye Movement Desensitization and Reprocessing (EMDR) therapy, discussed in more detail on page 181.

- **Alternately contracting thigh/buttocks muscles**—I squeeze/contract left thigh and/or buttocks, relax, and then contract right thigh/buttocks muscles. I repeat for a minute or two.

- **Alternating foot pressure on a perpendicular surface**—I lie on a bed with a footboard and press one foot against the footboard and then the other foot, repeating for a minute. Another option is lying on the floor and pressing feet against a wall. This helps when I awaken with anxiety.
- **Cross-body motions**—These include crawling on floor; shifting right shoulder/elbow toward left hip/knee and left shoulder/elbow toward right hip/knee; and creating an infinity sign (∞) with hands, arms, feet, hips, or torso while sitting, standing, or lying down. I also enhance yoga poses with movements that alternate left and right as well as criss-crossing my arms through the space in front of the midline of my body during the flow of poses.
- **Alternate nostril breathing**—A practice from yoga traditions. I inhale through left nostril while holding the right nostril closed. Then I exhale through the right while my left nostril is closed. Next, I inhale through my right nostril while the left nostril remains closed. Finally, I exhale through the left while the right is closed. I repeat the cycle several times.
- **Swimming**
- **Biking**
- **Painting**—I can paint by alternating using left and right hands, alternating creating painting motions toward the left with motions to the right, or through following an alternating pattern with my eyes.
- **EMDR**—Eye Movement Desensitization and Reprocessing therapy, see details in the "Getting Help from Others" chapter on page 181.
- **LENS**—Low Energy Neurofeedback System, see details in the "Getting Help from Others" chapter on page 182.

- **Journaling**—Perhaps using writing portions of brain while also being aware of body sensations and emotions helps with brain flexibility.
- **BodyTalk**—Energy balancing healing system, see details in the "Getting Help from Others" chapter on page 184.
- **Self-talk/affirmations**—A way to "re-parent" my wounded parts, supportive self-talk means I am aware of what's going on within me in the present moment, even if it's created by old patterns from abuse. Sometimes it feels good to speak to my inner parts by saying "you." Other times, using "I" or "we" or "our" feels most healing. *I believe you* (to young part). *I am innocent. I love you. I am okay. It's okay. I understand myself. You've done nothing wrong. Our feelings are welcome. My body speaks to me.*
- **Herbs for nervous system support**—I consulted an experienced herbalist.
- **Word searches**—I bought a book of word searches and found that scanning right to left for letters, and then switching directions, and repeating this several times helps with shifting out of uncomfortable feelings, similar to EMDR and brain training games.

Your Notes

Cleansing

Sexual violation leaves traces in the body, which can feel "gross." There's no better term for it—gross and needing to be washed off. The discomfort varies in texture, color, and temperature: slimy, rough, sharp, hot, cold, slippery, red, brown, orange, dark green. It shows up in body sensations, in emotions, and in thoughts.

My self-care approach can be direct, as in a spot-specific salt scrub or warm compress. Other times the areas of grossness feel cleansed when associated emotions or thoughts are noticed and allowed expression. These are techniques that work well for me in cleansing body and mind:

- **Salt scrub**—In the shower, I mix a little water with coarse or fine sea salt and gently scrub any areas that feel uncomfortable, often my stomach, pelvis, or upper chest. I may add olive oil or herbs from my garden to the salt mixture. I scrub briefly, for less than a minute, to avoid damaging my skin. Then I rinse it off.
- **Salt bath**—I add a half to one cup of sea salt (coarse or fine) to the bath for a five- to twenty-minute soak. I also add in herbs and flowers for aroma and whimsy. I love putting in long rosemary sprigs from my garden. If I stay too long in the water, though, then I may feel too floaty and dissociated.
- **Mud**—Sticking my hands or feet into mud, especially clay mud, feels as though it pulls out uncomfortable sensations from all over my body. I use mud in nature or my yard. Clay can also be purchased from body care stores.
- **Bathing feet or body in stream or river**—Flowing water feels more cleansing to me than more stationary water.
- **Acupressure self-care routines**—*Acupressure for Emotional Healing* by Michael Reed Gach and Beth Ann Henning

outlines many routines to tend various emotions and conditions, including anxiety, sexual abuse, PTSD, and chronic fatigue.

- **Forest bathing**—The Japanese have a term, *shinrin-yoku,* that translates as "forest bathing." The concept resonates deeply with me, as I find much relief, comfort, and invigoration when I spend time in the woods.
- **Breath of fire**—A yogic breathing technique in which the abdomen, especially near the diaphragm, is rapidly pulled inward toward the spine while exhaling quickly through the nose. The inhalations naturally follow the exhalations. Rapid repetition for a minute leaves me feeling more energized and free from feeling invaded. To keep from feeling ungrounded, I envision the energy flowing inward and downward.
- **Candles**—Candlelight comforts me. I like the chemical-free beeswax votive candles. As I write this book, very often I have a candle lit next to the laptop. It feels like an encouraging companion.
- **Aromatherapy**—I choose essential oils based on what I'm drawn to and how I feel after smelling the oil. Eucalyptus, frankincense, rosemary, cedarwood, and clary sage work well for a variety of my symptoms. A combination of frankincense, marjoram, and grapefruit eases my anxiety patterns. I add them to salt baths. I also have a small clay necklace pendant that can hold a couple drops. Essential oil diffusers provide a roomful of scent.
- **Smudging**—I clear the energy of a room or around my body with the smoke from sacred herbs such as sage, sweetgrass, and cedar.
- **Hot/cool compresses**—Great for headaches, pelvis pain, chest restriction, and muscle tension, compresses help not

Your Notes

CLEANSING

Your Notes

only by boosting circulation (hot and cool) or easing inflammation (cool) but also by providing a sensory input that counters the trauma pattern feelings in the body.

- **Crying/screaming/venting out any sounds**
- **Singing and chanting**—Singing songs can uplift or shake me clear of what I want to let go of. Chanting cleanses as sound vibrations flow within me and out of me. Two of my favorites are the soothing Vedic Gayatri mantra and a powerhouse clearing Tibetan mantra of Hung Vajra Peh. Deva Premal and Mark Stanton Welch are two musicians with lovely collections of mantras.
- **Building a fire**—Tending a fire can empower and comfort me. Sometimes I build one with the intention of letting it help me tap into some needed fiery emotions. I also benefit from writing down emotions or situations and then burning the paper to help me clear the problems.
- **Cleansing/calming foods**—When my body held a lot of nausea, there were three foods that felt most cleansing: white potatoes, oatmeal, and green apples. To shift out of heavy grief feelings or brain fog, sharp or bitter flavors worked well: radishes, hot peppers, kale, turnip greens, citrus, and turmeric.
- **Herbal teas**—Making and sipping tea can be a calming routine. Some nervous system supportive herbs, such as tulsi and lemon balm, are frequently in my cup. Mint and fennel teas are my favorites for soothing an upset stomach. Many of my garden herbs make lovely teas from fresh herbs: rosemary, lemon balm, oregano, and mint.
- **Avoiding certain people or crowds**—Understanding that other people's moods and even thoughts can impact me was a major turning point in my healing. If I felt drained or

emotionally triggered during or after seeing a person, even if it seemed a friendly exchange, I needed to trust my responses and avoid them if possible. People exchange energy, and when I am feeling too open or vulnerable, I need to cocoon myself to heal. Being a hermit at times has been part of my healing journey.

- **Resting**
- **Journaling**
- **Dancing**—I benefit from adding in some cross-body, left–right motions as well as some good stomping.
- **Tidying up the house**—Having at least one tidy room helps me feel more balanced and energetic in general.
- **Pulling weeds/trimming in the garden**
- **Walking, sitting, or gardening in the rain**—Raindrops cool and clear me.
- **Colored light meditation**—I visualize uncomfortable feelings/thoughts leaving my body and being replaced by comforting or vibrant colors of light. Sometimes simultaneously I physically move my hands over an area and create a pulling out or brushing off motion.
- **Saying no or yes in congruence with my authentic promptings**—A verbal way of creating boundaries and shifting out anything that needs to be cleansed. "No, you don't get to dump on me," and "Yes, I have the right to decide what works for me.

Your Notes

SURVIVOR'S TOOLBOX

How to Choose Self-Care

I've described many self-care options. You may be wondering how to determine which to use and when. I believe honing your own intuitive guidance in each moment is ultimately the most effective path for healing. Here's a general map though for where my intuition usually takes me to cope moment by moment.

WATCH inwardly   DESCRIBE sensations
LISTEN for thoughts   LABEL emotions

Sometimes this step of being aware is all that's needed to comfort and shift out of distress.

DO self-care

First, try self-talk. Speak comfortingly to yourself, affirming that it's okay to be feeling all that you are feeling.

Second, ask yourself, "What do I need?" When I reach for my intuition, I imagine asking a younger version of myself if that feels like where the pain is coming from.

Then sit quietly and listen. A thought might pop into your mind about specific self-care. Or you may notice a change in body sensations, so choose self-care that is directed at that body region.

CLEANSING techniques (see page 170) are a good final step in self-care after moving through difficult emotions.

TALK to a friend or a therapist when you feel like you need human connection or help from someone else.

Not much time for Self-Care:

- Butterfly hug (page 167)
- Hand mudras (page 165)
- EFT (page 184)
- Breath of fire (page 171)

- Upbeat music
- Dancing (page 173)
- Movement (page 183)
- Distractions

More time for Self-Care:

What is the dominant distress feeling?

	Off-balance, Less Aware of Certain Body Areas	Spacey, Mental Fog, Anxiety	Big Emotions, Thoughts or Memories of Trauma	Feeling Invaded, Heavy, Coated with Icky Energy
Choose:	REBALANCING Techniques (page 167)	DEEP PRESSURE Techniques (page 161)	GROUNDING Techniques (page 164) & PAINTING	CLEANSING Techniques (page 170)

To choose from within the list of each category of techniques from earlier in this chapter, go down the list and pause at each possible technique. Notice how you feel inside when imagining doing that technique. Try techniques that give you solid, comforting, supported, or positive feelings.

Common order of self-care for me as I cycle through various distress feelings:

Deep Pressure, then Grounding/Emotional expression, then Rebalancing, and, finally, Cleansing.

SURVIVOR'S TOOLBOX

Creating Self-Care Reminders

Find ways to document what helps you feel better when symptoms appear. When dealing with the onset of anxiety or some other trauma symptom, I often found myself forgetting the options for caring for myself that I'd already used in the past. "Trauma brain," a fogginess and hopelessness, could easily prevent me from turning to self-care techniques. I simply couldn't remember what to do. Or I could remember some but not all of my options. I had trouble gathering myself together to figure out what might work best in that moment. Making a list or visual reminder of what has worked in the past can give some subtle encouragement that these feelings or thoughts won't stay around forever.

Simple List

Start a list of self-care techniques that soothe or shift any unwanted emotions, moods, thoughts, or physical sensations. Have it in a location that is usually accessible to you: a small notebook you carry in a purse or briefcase, the last pages in your journal, or as a document on your computer or phone. Keep track of symptoms experienced and the specific care that helped. You may also find a benefit to noting the date and time of day, plus any triggers you can identify. This can help identify patterns in your healing process.

Deck of Cards

List each technique on an index card. Add in decoration and notes about how it's helped. When you have no idea how to feel better, choose a card blindly from the deck and try that technique.

Poster

Enhance your simple list by transferring it to poster board. Decorate it with markers, paint, photos, glitter, magazine images, etc. Beyond reminding you of how to help yourself feel better, these colors and images can serve as a healing anchor for you each time you reach for the poster. Save room on the poster for future additions.

Basket

Gather items you frequently use for self-care into a central spot, such as in a basket in your bedroom. Place your journal, paper and markers for sketching, aromatherapy essential oils, lotions, affirmation cards, photos of loved ones, a soft shawl, and any other items of support into the basket. Simply holding the basket may bring a sense of support and comfort. It shows you that you love you.

Body Map

Honor the truth of what your body has to tell you. When you are feeling symptoms, draw and paint a small or life-size map of your body and what you feel within. If you want to create a life-size map of your body, use a long piece of butcher paper or staple three poster boards together. Have a friend trace your outline as you lie on the paper. Let your intuition guide you to colors, shapes, and patterns that best represent your inner sensations and emotions. Use markers, colored pencils, and paint. Paste images or even three-dimensional objects onto the map of yourself. You may want to create a front and a back map. After creating the map of what you feel currently, create a map representing how you'd like to feel. These maps can be great places to document self-care techniques specific to certain areas of the body.

Getting Help from Others

What I Look for in a Helping Professional

Especially in early years of healing, I needed much help from professionals, from psychologists and doctors to yoga instructors and herbalists. I eventually came to understand that the most helpful professionals show three general characteristics within their practices: they have extensive knowledge of trauma, they communicate clearly about therapies and techniques, and they are adept at integrating my internal, in-the-moment experiences into the consultation or therapy.

Trauma-Informed Practices

Professionals who understand the impacts of trauma provide emotionally safer care for victims of sexual violence. For me, it's a red flag if a professional has very little to say or responds uncomfortably to my disclosure that I am healing from sexual abuse. Victims of abuse need professionals who understand the courage it can take to trust a professional. We need them to be knowledgeable about the potential needs of a survivor, including how to respond sensitively if we become triggered and start to dissociate. For example, I need practitioners who understand and honor my request that, whenever possible, I want to avoid the trigger of lying flat on my back. Rape culture influences professionals, too, and it's vital that anyone working with survivors is very careful to monitor their comments for any victim-doubting or victim-blaming connotations. A sadly significant portion of my journals is home to my pain from the secondary trauma from several ignorant, dismissive, or blaming "helping" professionals. Many professions now have trainings that teach trauma-informed practices. Given the prevalence of all types of abuse and trauma, I think they should be mandatory.

Ongoing Informed Consent

At the core of sexual violence, a victim's human rights are shredded. When seeking help to heal, a victim deserves to be educated about the therapy or treatment and to be given choices whenever possible. I look for a professional who communicates before, during, and after consultations or sessions. Informed consent doesn't end once you've signed the intake forms and waiver. A practitioner must verbally check

Choosing Help Wisely

You are the customer. This is your time, money, and health. You get to use your discernment to find a good fit.

- Familiarize yourself with signs of good therapy as well as red flag lists from GoodTherapy.org and *Resurrection After Rape* by Matt Atkinson. Apply these in sessions not only with psychologists and counselors but with all conventional and alternative health practitioners who are helping you address trauma symptoms.
- Consider asking for details of the practitioner's trainings in working with trauma victims. Ask what books/websites they'd recommend for survivors. Ask what accommodations they've made in the past in consultations with victims. They should be able to list some.
- Especially for doctors, dentists, and others who won't directly be treating you for trauma healing, consider giving the practitioner a brochure describing victims' needs, as a way to broach the topic of any specific needs you have when receiving care. One option is *Trauma Survivors in Medical and Dental Settings* by The Western Massachusetts Training Consortium.[1]
- Monitor a practitioner's responses to your questions for the level of comfort they display. If a question makes them uneasy, then they may not navigate a real-life triggered moment well.
- Look up the practitioner on licensing board websites for information on prior complaints or sanctions. While many have benefited greatly from therapies that fall in the category of alternative medicine, some modalities do not have the consumer protection of extensive training requirements, state licensure, and ethics review boards. In these cases—and really, in any treatment situation—it's crucial that you use discernment and monitor the sessions for red flags that may derail therapeutic progress—and could cause more damage.

---

1   http://www.integration.samhsa.gov/clinical-practice/Trauma_Survivors_in_Medical_and_Dental_Settings.pdf

in, seek feedback, and be willing to pause or change the treatment if possible. I realize this often adds time to therapies and doesn't fit well with tightly scheduled professions, but it's necessary to provide respectful care to victims without traumatizing them further.

Weaves Client's Inner Awareness into Sessions

Some practitioners have fairly rigid protocols for their therapeutic techniques. In my healing, these stringent systems felt unhelpful or invasive. Building upon the practice of maintaining ongoing informed consent, a practitioner can use a client's inner experience of emotions, body sensations, and thoughts to choose or guide techniques. Traumatic experiences left me feeling like I'm not in charge of my life. Therapeutic interventions that empower me through listening and responding sensitively to what is happening within me work most effectively for me.

Therapies I've Found Helpful

Talk Therapy

Especially in early years of healing, I needed talk therapy for help in unsilencing me and lifting away self-blame. Because of the intensity of the topic, I couldn't rely on very many friends or family to be able to listen to what I was going through. I needed a skilled therapist to be a grounded witness and compassionate guide. I learned much from therapists who utilized Internal Family Systems Therapy, ego-state therapy, and inner-child therapy. These approaches teach skills that translate easily into self-care.

EMDR

I don't think I could have made great strides in moving through trauma without Eye Movement Desensitization and Reprocessing (EMDR) therapy. Very often, I requested EMDR in the second half of my talk therapy sessions. While I maintained awareness of the emotional pain, memories, or physical sensations stirred up within me, my therapist slowly moved her hand back and forth from left to right and back again, over and over, as I followed her movements with my eyes. We'd pause when

I'd feel a shift, as my emotions or thoughts or sensations changed, sometimes seemingly draining out of me. If new feelings arose to be tended, we'd do multiple rounds of EMDR. Sister techniques that rely on bilateral stimulation and dual attention (attention on the distress inside as well as on the left/right input) also have a similar trauma distress processing feeling to me. The butterfly hug and other left/right alternating techniques, described on pages 167–169 in the "Building a Foundation of Creative Self-Care" chapter, are ways I brought EMDR's healing power out of the therapy hour and into my daily life. See the Survivor's Toolbox: Creatively Exploring Body, Brain, and Soul Connections on page 186 for descriptions on other EMDR-inspired self-care tools. For survivors in intense healing phases, it is wise to receive EMDR with an experienced trauma therapist before branching out into EMDR-inspired self-care.

LENS

The Low Energy Neurofeedback System (LENS) is a type of neurofeedback that I found highly effective for helping me shake free from mental fog, fatigue and full-body pain patterns. I also credit LENS with helping me to more easily shift out of distress when triggered. It's as though this neurofeedback therapy enabled my brain signals to not dive quite as deep in the grooves formed by trauma. Neurofeedback involves having a computer system monitor brain waves through sensors on the scalp.[20] Choosing to seek out LENS therapy was an early lesson in following my intuition. The psychologist I was seeing had recommended traditional neurofeedback, but when I read a small section on LENS in the book *A Symphony in the Brain* by Jim Robbins, I felt a strong inner pull toward trying it. I'm glad I did.

Somatic Experiencing

I learned some wonderfully helpful skills from therapists trained in Somatic Experiencing. By tracking body sensations, I was able to discern more about how my past traumas were impacting me physiologically, especially through my nervous system stuck in the "freeze" mode of "fight/flight/freeze." Somatic Experiencing methods

20 For more information, see www.ochslabs.com.

then offer subtle body movements that help the body get unstuck from trauma modes. Like EMDR, this is a helpful additional skill for a talk therapist to employ for trauma resolution.[21]

Movement Therapies

Yoga, tai chi, qigong, and Continuum Movement are powerful ways to cultivate inner awareness of physical, emotional, mental, and spiritual health. Classes are sometimes offered specifically for trauma survivors. Trauma healing can be supported by shifting tension patterns in the body, balancing left and right sides, encouraging core strength, and helping to fully inhabit the body. The spiritual aspects of these practices become most apparent to me when I feel my life force (chi/qi) flowing more freely. My spirit comes home to my body. Some days, trauma patterns made me feel too open and vulnerable, so following along in a class that encouraged pushing past edges wasn't healing for me. I needed more restorative poses. Individual consultations worked best for me during times that I needed safety and privacy for allowing strong emotions to flow.

Touch Therapies & Energy Healing

Massage therapy, BodyTalk, EFT, acupressure, polarity therapy, Breema, craniosacral therapy, and reiki are the touch and energy healing therapies I've relied upon. Receiving touch can be a very complicated trigger for survivors of sexual violence. It took me a while to understand that the touch therapies that were part of my professional life and which had helped me relax so much in the past were, for a time, counterproductive for my healing. I had to stop receiving touch therapies for a couple of years in order to let my nervous system relax and let go of touch as a strong trauma trigger. There are some trauma-informed trainings, such as Trauma Touch Therapy, which can help massage therapists learn to more sensitively and effectively work with survivors.

---

21 Other body-oriented psychotherapies can be researched at the United States Association for Body Psychotherapy website, www.usabp.org.

BodyTalk

The BodyTalk System was a good fit for me because I could receive it fully clothed and seated, eliminating several trauma triggers. This healing system also feels very respectful by incorporating the wisdom of the client's body, through the use of applied kinesiology, to help guide sessions. BodyTalk Access classes are a good introduction to learn self-care techniques.[22]

EFT

I learned EFT, the Emotional Freedom Techniques, from a talk therapist. Soon I could use it on my own to help when I felt overwhelmed emotionally. In general, it involves gentle tapping on specific points of the meridian system referenced in acupuncture. It's easy to find information online about the protocol and how to use it at home. Many other similar tapping methods for emotional, mental, physical, and spiritual health are springing up too. On days when I find the tapping over-stimulating and/or irritating, a single gentle touch or massage on the same points is also effective for me.

Chiropractic

When my stretching and yoga practice doesn't help with muscle tension and body alignments, I go to a chiropractor. Just as with other therapies that involve touch, I needed to take a break from this type of treatment for a couple of years. Even when I wanted a chiropractor's help, having someone pushing and pulling on my body felt too invasive. Network Spinal Analysis is a form of chiropractic care that is gentler, working with the subtle energy of the body. I've found it to be preferable to traditional chiropractic therapies when I needed to be treated very sensitively.

Acupuncture

Acupuncture, especially "Five Element" acupuncture, assisted me in moving through some stuck emotional patterns. However, my skin/touch ultra-sensitivities made receiving acupuncture difficult during intense healing times.

22 Tutorials for the brain/body balancing "Cortices Technique" can be found online at www.bodytalksystem.com.

Herbal Medicine

I consulted with an experienced, well-trained herbalist. For a couple of years, I took restorative herbs focused on the nervous system, which helped tremendously without the side effects I'd felt with some anti-anxiety medication. During times of high stress, I still may take them. I grow lemon balm, rosemary, and tulsi to make my own calming and mind-clearing teas.

Physicians

I prefer consulting with doctors who fully embrace that mental health is connected to physical health. Integrative health centers are great places to find doctors who want to pay attention to their patients as a whole person. I relied on the help of a physician for trauma healing during intense phases, when I needed anti-depressant and anti-anxiety medications.

For More Information

There are so many types of mental health and body-oriented therapies that can help survivors of trauma. For a more comprehensive list, see the "Selecting Your Interventions" chapter in this book:

Healing from Trauma by Jasmin Lee Cori

SURVIVOR'S TOOLBOX

Creatively Exploring Body, Brain, and Soul Connections

If you are in an intense healing phase from trauma or if you start to feel overwhelmed when trying these techniques, I recommend working first with an EMDR therapist for a period of time before using these at-home, EMDR-inspired self-care techniques.

Inspired by the back and forth, left to right movements of EMDR (see page 181), I started painting with my fingertips, slowly trailing to the right and then to the left. I repeated this motion with various colors. My eyes softly gazed at my fingers and at the blending colors, tracking the back and forth movements. I used my left hand and then switched to my right hand. I find the effects of this type of painting to be very similar to that of EMDR.

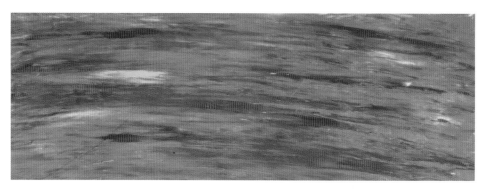

Emotions resolve. Thoughts let go of me. Peace returns to my body.

One day, I realized that when I moved my eyes in patterns besides the left-to-right strategy of EMDR, I also felt therapeutic inner shifting. An EFT protocol includes some movements of the eyes in circles, so I tried that. Then I tried zigzags. And spirals. I liked the combination of the circle movements and the left-to-right zigzags so I created this piece of yarn art from rainbow yarn glued onto paper. It's about 18 inches wide, so I can set it out in

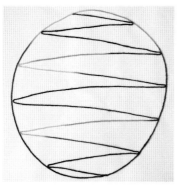

front of me and follow the pattern with a soft, unfocused gaze. The color changes help me stay with the yarn path and seem to encourage change within. I can start at the bottom, top, or anywhere in the middle. I can go clockwise or counterclockwise. When I feel an intensification of symptoms, I hold my eyes in that position and allow a pause, a practice inspired by David Grand's book *Brainspotting*. Often, I add in a butterfly hug (see page 167) during this pause to help process the emotion or sensation.

Just as eye movements with inner awareness can impact our internal state, so can other intentional movements of our bodies. I am fortunate to have several labyrinths for contemplative prayer near my home. I feel as though walking through a labyrinth is also a walk within myself. Sometimes through the crevices of my heart. Sometimes in the dark and light folds of my mind. Walking seems to symbolize meeting new challenges and letting go of what I need to leave behind. When I don't have time to walk in a labyrinth, I can create a finger labyrinth. Tracing through the paths with my finger or pen can be as powerful as walking a labyrinth.

Resources

National Sexual Assault Hotline, 1-800-656-4673

National Sexual Assault Online Hotline www.rainn.org

National Suicide Prevention Lifeline, 1-800-273-8255

Or chat online: www.suicidepreventionlifeline.org

Healing from Sexual Violence & Trauma

The Courage to Heal by Ellen Bass and Laura Davis

The Courage to Heal Workbook by Laura Davis

Resurrection After Rape by Matt Atkinson

The Body Keeps the Score: Brain, Mind, and Body in the Healing of Trauma by Bessel van der Kolk

Healing from Trauma by Jasmin Lee Cori

EMDR Institute, Inc., www.emdr.com

GoodTherapy.Org, www.goodtherapy.org

American Art Therapy Association, www.arttherapy.org

The Body Remembers: The Psychophysiology of Trauma and Trauma Treatment by Babette Rothschild

Trauma and Recovery by Judith Herman

Trauma and Memory: Brain and Body in a Search for the Living Past: A Practical Guide for Understanding and Working with Traumatic Memory by Peter A. Levine

Waking the Tiger: Healing Trauma by Peter A. Levine

Healing Trauma: A Pioneering Program for Restoring the Wisdom of Your Body by Peter A. Levine

Trauma-Proofing Your Kids by Peter Levine and Maggie Kline

United States Association for Body Psychotherapy, www.usabp.org

The Body Bears the Burden: Trauma, Dissociation, and Disease by Robert Scaer

I Can't Get Over It: A Handbook for Trauma Survivors by Aphrodite Matsakis

Repressed Memories: A Journey to Recovery from Sexual Abuse by Renee Fredrickson

Healing the Traumatized Self: Consciousness Neuroscience Treatment by Paul Frewen and Ruth Lanius

When Survivors Give Birth: Understanding and Healing the Effects of Early Sexual Abuse on Childbearing Women by Penny Simkin and Phyllis Klaus

Searching for Angela Shelton, a film by Angela Shelton, www.searchingforangelashelton.com

The Sexual Healing Journey: A Guide for Survivors of Sexual Abuse by Wendy Maltz

Rape, Abuse & Incest National Network, www.rainn.org

Pandora's Project: Support and resources for survivors of rape and sexual abuse, www.pandys.org

Figuring Out What Is Up with My Nervous System

The Brain That Changes Itself by Norman Doidge

The Brain's Way of Healing by Norman Doidge

My Stroke of Insight by Jill Bolte Taylor

Change Your Brain, Change Your Body by Daniel G. Amen

Unleash the Power of the Female Brain by Daniel G. Amen

A Symphony in the Brain by Jim Robbins

The Healing Power of Neurofeedback by Stephen Larsen

Too Loud Too Bright Too Fast Too Tight: What to Do If You Are Sensory Defensive in an Overstimulating World by Sharon Heller

Quiet: The Power of Introverts in a World That Can't Stop Talking by Susan Cain

The Highly Sensitive Person by Elaine Aron, www.hsperson.com

Consent, Power Dynamics, and Sexual Abuse by Trusted Professionals

AdvocateWeb, www.advocateweb.org

Love Does No Harm: Sexual Ethics for the Rest of Us by Marie M. Fortune

Sex in the Forbidden Zone: When Men in Power—Therapists, Doctors, Clergy, Teachers, and Others—Betray Women's Trust by Peter Rutter

At Personal Risk: Boundary Violations in Professional-Client Relationships by Marilyn R. Peterson

Sexual Abuse by Health Professionals by P. Susan Penfold

Alternative Healing

Acupressure's Potent Points by Michael Reed Gach

Acupressure for Emotional Healing by Michael Reed Gach and Beth Ann Henning

Mudras: Yoga in Your Hands by Gertrud Hirschi

Neurofeedback website specific to Low Energy Neurofeedback System (LENS), www.ochslabs.com

Energy Medicine by Donna Eden and David Feinstein

Energy Medicine for Women by Donna Eden and David Feinstein

Energy Tapping for Trauma by Fred P. Gallo

Brainspotting by David Grand

The Book of Ayurveda by Judith H. Morrison

Emotional Freedom Techniques, www.emofree.com

Inspiration, Creativity, and Activism

The Complete Artist's Way by Julia Cameron

Rememberings and Celebrations: Loving Reminders of the Great Mother's Voice, Cards by Robyn L. Posin, www.compassionateink.com, www.forthelittleonesinside.com

Trust Your Vibes by Sonia Choquette

Painted Prayers by Jody Uttal

Inspiration Sandwich: Stories to Inspire Our Creative Freedom by SARK

Make Your Creative Dreams Real by SARK

Writing Down the Bones: Freeing the Writer Within by Natalie Goldberg

SoulCollage, www.soulcollage.com

Center for Touch Drawing, www.touchdrawing.com

In the Body of the World by Eve Ensler

Yogini: The Power of Women in Yoga by Janice Gates

Spiritual Housecleaning by Kathryn L. Robyn

Big Magic: Creative Living Beyond Fear by Elizabeth Gilbert

Nonviolent Communication by Marshall B. Rosenberg

The Creative Activist by Rae Luskin

The Woman's Comfort Book by Jennifer Louden

The Woman's Retreat Book by Jennifer Louden

The Couple's Comfort Book by Jennifer Louden

World-Wide Labyrinth Locator, www.labyrinthlocator.com

Thank You

To all of the supporters of my publishing crowdfunding campaign. Your generosity fueled this project and gave me much encouragement.

To Laura Zats and the whole team at Wise Ink Creative Publishing. You saw my vision clearly and helped me bring it into the world.

To my editor, Ally Bishop, for her hard work and the magical reshuffling of the book's content.

To Ryan Scheife of Mayfly Design for creating a beautiful and inviting design to house my words and images.

To Ed Schmookler for your helpful feedback on an early version of the manuscript.

To the Orange County Rape Crisis Center, United Church of Chapel Hill, Carrboro Yoga Company, and Hillsborough Yoga for hosting art shows of my paintings.

To all the teachers and therapists, especially Barbara, Robyn, Chitra, Carol, Libby, Edie, Carey and Sonia, who guided me in finding my way toward healing.

To all my friends, neighbors, and family for being my community of support, especially Kaselehlia, Carrie, Caroline, Jennie, Jim, and Kath.

To Bonnie, Genevieve, Judy, Sridevi, Yvette, Jean, and Nancy for encircling me with kindness and love.

To Chelsea and Linda for their friendship, understanding, input, and encouragement.

To my son for his humor, creativity, and joy.

To Sarah, my sister/editor/friend, for patiently clearing away my doubts and fears whenever they surfaced. Your clarity, strength, and love have nurtured me throughout my healing and the creation of this book.

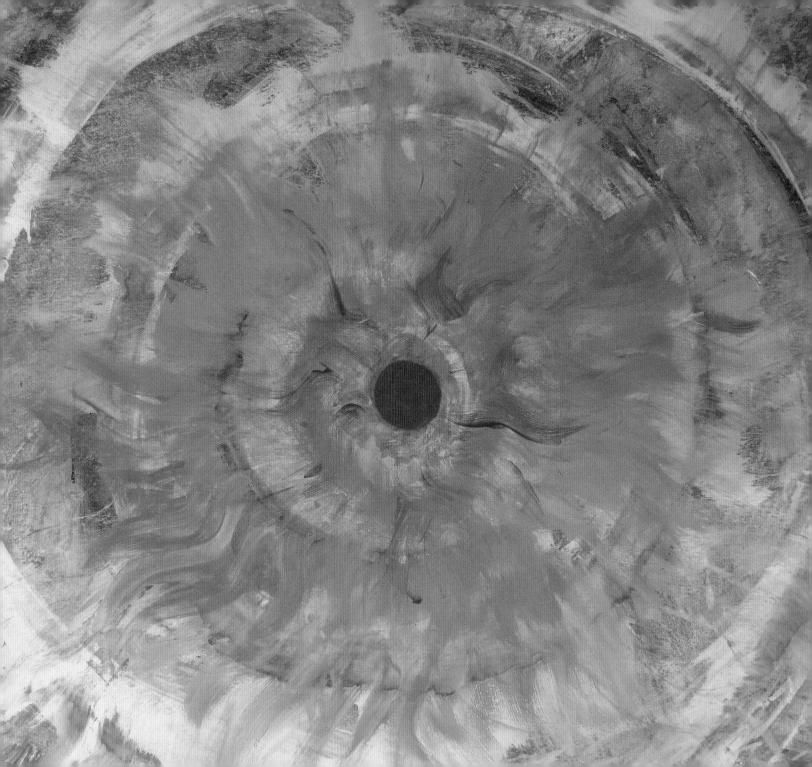

Ripple Effects

I send out prayer ripples for:

Greater understanding and compassion for victims and all they go through.
Greater openness for victims to share their experiences without shame.
Greater resources to help trauma victims heal.
Greater awareness of how power dynamics play a role in abuse scenarios.
Greater efforts toward healing trauma in people to heal violence among people and toward nature.
Greater respect for the impacts our ways of being have on ourselves, others, and our planet.
Reconnection to ourselves, each other, and the earth.